Staying Cool and In Control:
A Behaviorist's Guide for Parents

Dr. Roger McIntire

Summit Crossroads Press
Columbia, Maryland

Copyright 2016 Summit Crossroads Press

All rights reserved. No portion of this book may be reproduced mechanically, electronically, or by any other means, including photocopying, without written permission from Summit Crossroads Press.

Summit Crossroads Press books are available at a discount when purchased in bulk for premiums, promotions, fund-raising or educational use. For more information, contact the Marketing Department at:
    Summit Crossroads Press
    9329 Angelina Circle
    Columbia, MD 21045
    SumCross@aol.com
    www.parentsuccess.com

ISBN 978-0-9834049-8-9

LCCN 2016914831

Cover by Six Penny Graphics, Fredericksburg, VA.

All names in the parent-child examples and not connected with published research are fictitious and do not refer to any person living or dead.

Published by Summit Crossroads Press, Columbia, MD, USA.

About the Author

Dr. Roger McIntire, father of three, has taught child psychology and principles in family counseling and therapy at the University of Maryland for 32 years. He is the author of many books including *Raising Good Kids in Tough Times, Raising Your Teenager, Enjoy Successful Parenting, For Love of Children, Child Psychology* (a college text), *Teenagers and Parents,* and *College Keys: Getting In, Doing Well, Avoiding the 4 Big Mistakes.*

In addition to his work with families, Dr. McIntire has been a consultant and teacher of teachers in preschools, grade schools, high schools, and colleges. He has published research articles concerning infant vocalizations, eating problems, strategies in elementary school teaching, and high school motivation. He also published several studies of college drop-outs during his tenure as Associate Dean for Undergraduate Students at the University of Maryland.

What Every Parent Should Know About Raising Children is an extensive revision of both *Raising Good Kids in Tough Times* and *Enjoy Successful Parenting*. It is the result of McIntire's decades of experiences as a counselor, parent, web editor, columnist, and grandparent during the 13 years since those two books were published.

The Summit Crossroads Press Series
by Dr. Roger McIntire

TEENAGERS & PARENTS:
   12 Steps to a Better Relationship

RAISING YOUR TEENAGER
   5 Crucial Skills for Moms and Dads, 2010

RAISING GOOD KIDS IN TOUGH TIMES
   7 Crucial Habits for Parent Success, 1999
   (also published in Korea, Thailand)

COLLEGE KEYS
   Getting In, Doing Well, Avoiding the 4 Big Mistakes, 1998

ENJOY SUCCESSFUL PARENTING
   Practical Strategies for Parents of Children 2-12, 1997

TEENAGERS AND PARENTS
   10 Steps to a Better Relationship,
   (Revised in: 1991, 1996, 1998 and 2000)
   (also published in Brazil, Germany, Croatia, Korea, Slovenia, Serbia)

Table of Contents

Preface   9
Chapter One: "Mom/Dad, Can We Talk?"   13
    "Yeah, Good Morning, Don't Talk to Me."   13
    Routines for Talking and Listening   14
    Five Cautions: Beware the "Quick Fixes" and the "Games"   21
    EXERCISE: Practice These Listening Skills and Cautions in Family
        Conversation   34

Chapter Two: Dealing with Problems at Home and at School   37
    The Basic Three   40
    The Challenge of Attention-Getting Behavior   45
    The Challenge of a Child Becoming a Student   55
    Strategies for Tests   61
    The Computer Revolution in School   62
    Tips About Social Problems   65
    EXERCISE: To Observe What's Happening, Start a Behavior Chart   67

Chapter Three: "I Love You" is Not Much Without "I Like You"   69
    Passing on Social Skills   72
    Have Your Support at the Ready   76
    Learning to Practice; Practicing to Learn   83
    While Pursuing Perfection, What Happens to "Liking"?   88
    "I Always Felt I Was Never Quite Good Enough"   91
    "Paying No Attention" Requires a Plan   94
    EXERCISE: Fill In These Important Lists of Priorities   97

Chapter Four: Bad Habits in Childhood   99
    The S.A.D. Behaviors: Sex, Alcohol, and Drugs   99
    Battery-Operated Security Blankets   101
    The "Boy Problem"   104
    The Driving Threat   107

The Bad Movie Problem 108
When Should Your Child Start Smoking? 110
Battle of the Bulge 111
"Mom. I think I have a Problem" 113
Who's to Blame? 114
Values learned through Family Connections 116
The Dangers of Inside Blames 119
What About Chris? What About Aaron? 123
Routines That Lead to Self-Confidence and Self-Esteem 126
What Will Make You Happy? 127
"Character? The Subject Never Came Up!" 128

Chapter Five: Caution, the Children are Watching 131
She's Just Like Her Mom 131
Learned Dispositions 136
What is Good Behavior and Where Can I Get Some? 140
How Much Explanation is Required for Children? 141
"Tiger Mom's" Model 143
Trophy Children 145

Chapter Six: Discipline: You Can't Make a Garden By Just Pulling Weeds 149
Uncle Harry's Hard Line Won't Help 150
Why Uncle Harry is Wrong 150
Correcting the Course 158
Avoid Rules That Only Work Once 162
Isn't Adulthood Great? Alternatives to Punishment 163
The Complication of Negative Reinforcement 172
The Work of Being a Parent 175
EXERCISE: A Planning Session Agenda 175

Chapter Seven: Tips About Dealing with Almost Grown-Ups 179
Rule No. 1 for a Teenager Almost on His Own 179
Magical Thinking and How to Correct It 181
Your "Almost Grown Ups" Need Your Perspective 182
"Quit Treating Me Like a Child!": Eight Years Old and Going on 25 185
Bring In the Reinforcements 191
Parent Abuse: How Friends Can Hinder 193
Parent Teams: How Friends Can Help 195
College is Coming, Why Some Quit and Others Stay the Course 198

College Can Be a SNAP 199
Passing On Your Parenting Style 201
EXERCISE: Form a Parent Team: The Ground Rules 202
Extra Behavior Chart   205

Preface

This book is a combined revision of *Raising Good Kids in Tough Times*, published in *1999*, and *Enjoy Successful Parenting*, published in 1997. Since then, I have heard from over 600 parents who have sent questions to my website, ParentSuccess.com, and to behavior.org, the website for the Cambridge Center for Behavioral Studies. In answering these letters I have focused on possible family strategies to deal with tantrums, eating problems, sleeping difficulties, school problems, siblings, friends, and the numerous other problems of the growing-up years.

The practical strategies available in 1997 are still effective ones. We, that is, we psychologists and the parents we counsel, have perfected the basics and developed new approaches to many problems in the last decade. The most useful ones have been added in this revision.

TV and the ever-growing influence of the Internet's social network are sometimes dangerous to our children and teens. Along with the always-troublesome peer influence, we all struggle with the media's message to our kids from TV talk shows, movies, music, videos, and the Internet.

A parent's influence is also shared with teachers, soccer coaches, scout leaders, and music instructors—all vying for family time and influence.

As the model, coach, and disciplinarian, how can a parent hold steady in this hectic situation?

The seven chapters of this book will improve relationships in the family with hundreds of tips. The first three chapters deal with everyday parenting styles and routines that maintain parent-child relationships and make up the family atmosphere.

The next four chapters focus on the dangers of childhood, your model, your discipline issues, and finally, the way you deal with young adults. These discussions have parent happiness in mind first of all, your child's happiness second, and then her or his progress in growing up.

Your satisfaction and happiness come first because the best

prospect for your child's happiness is your satisfaction with the parenting job. Yet child-rearing has become more than a one- or two-person job. Parenting today is a tough challenge where many adults get in on the act, and we parents need to ask directly for their cooperation, not only from spouses, but also from teachers, relatives, friends, and guidance counselors at school.

Throughout the book, I use frequent examples and dialogues that are typical family interactions. The dialogues illustrate problems that can be resolved, but if not, they can accumulate to make a lot of unhappiness. Many surface at meal time:

"I don't want any of this stuff, it's icky!"

"Teri, those are fresh carrots and they're good for you."

"They look like poo."

"Don't talk like that! Eat your carrots and you can have dessert."

"Poo poo."

"Stop that. Eat your meat if you don't want carrots."

"All poo poo. Want cereal."

"This is not breakfast, Teri, and stop making a mess or you'll have to go to bed without supper!"

"Cereal! Daddy doesn't have any carrots."

"Take some carrots, George."

"No thanks."

"George!"

"What? Making me eat them won't help, maybe we should get out the cereal."

"Cereal, cereal, cereal!"

"Oh, all right, what's the use?"

Could Mom come up with any reaction that would get Teri to eat her carrots? Or should Mom let Teri do what she wants? How far can Mom stand to let that happen? Can Teri live on just cereal? If George did a better job helping out, would Teri be convinced?

And for good behavior (say, Teri eats a few carrots), Mom will encourage her—but how much encouragement is too much? Should she bribe Teri? In this situation, Mom's threats and warnings ("you'll go to bed without supper!") and bribes ("you can have dessert") produce a peculiar parent-child relationship and cloud Mom's real reasons for trying to get Teri to eat her carrots.

A good starting point would be a conversation between Mom and Dad about Teri's choices at supper. When both parents agree on the decision, they will find it easier to say, "This is what we're having for supper." Teri may not give up her demands right away, but all the talk about who is eating what will get less attention and that may make room for a better conversation and an improved family atmosphere.

At times, Teri would like Mom to believe she has no effect. She may even say so with the familiar, "You can't make me!" or "I don't care!" or just plain "No!" It's a child's way of struggling to make more room for herself under the umbrella of limits enforced by her parents.

A child's attempt to discourage a parent is a common scheme designed to weaken the opposition. Even adults, armies, and nations use this strategy: tell the opposition they are powerless.

Don't believe it. Children have their own personalities and go through their own stages, but your influence by example and reaction is always at work. Remember your parents and the influence they had on you, now that you can look back from a distance.

Most of the time, the suggestions and guidelines apply to both genders, and I hope you will understand if I dispense with the cumbersome "she or he" qualifier in most descriptions and instead use numerous specific examples of both genders.

The occasional exercises in this book give you opportunities to take an objective look at how your children are dealing with their family experiences and how you can maintain an enjoyable family life for yourself as well as for them. You'll be asked to review your priorities and consider the direction your strategies lead.

The ultimate goal of parenting is adult-rearing. Child-rearing is, of course, only a term for the steps along the way. We don't want little adults by tomorrow nor do we want our children to miss childhood. Our goal is for the children and the parents to enjoy their companionship during all the family years and feel a sense of pride when we realize the kids have become fine and competent adults.

A special message to Grandmas and Granddads

Many of us grandparents are looking for ways to help the next generation even though we are a step removed from the firing line. What's a grandpa or grandma to do in this time of so many differing family patterns from single parents to gay and lesbian parents to double parents, and every parent is very busy.

A century ago, we had no information highway interfering with the information flow from parent to child. We had few telephones, cars, or highways; and no televisions or computers, let alone Facebook and the Internet.

What a blessing that we have these things and yet what a burden. The really tough question is still tough—how to get along with each other. A grandparent's experience in this area can be a great help to a parent and the grandchildren in these tough times.

Don't be misled by the propaganda your sons and daughters now encounter from their kids that says parents have little influence on their own offspring or their grandchildren. Don't believe it. The habits described in this book can make a difference and they recycle through the family—you will help more family members than just the kids!

Grandparents can pick up the crucial habits, have an effect, and pass them along. Happily, we have these powerful habits available all the time: our listening, our support, our model, our observation, and our perspective on what's going on.

Chapter 1:
"Mom/Dad, Can We Talk?

If we meet someday and you tell me you used ideas from only one chapter in this book, I hope it is from this first chapter about listening and talking. Whether you have teens or toddlers, good communication will improve your fairness, influence, and negotiations described in all the coming chapters.

Good listening habits are also key to satisfying parent-child or parent-teen relationships. While parents look for opportunities to teach and to learn more about the experiences of their children, they need good skills.

Listening skills don't come naturally to most of us. But, with a little practice and extra attention, they will help you for the rest of your parenting years.

"Yeah, good morning, don't talk to me."

When you hear this important question, "Can we talk?" your first reaction is crucial. It can be encouraging or it can make a child regret asking. Since there is usually a problem behind the request, fragile feelings are likely to be just behind the problem.

When your son or daughter gets into a sour mood of silence because she or he feels vulnerable or possibly afraid of embarrassment—a very familiar situation for both children and teens—how can a parent be helpful without implying criticism? How can a child find a tolerant and uncritical ear and yet hear helpful suggestions?

Listening habits: Two ears and one mouth—just about the right ratio.

Most parents meet the requirement of experience, but to be heard, parents need to lead off with tolerance and avoid opinions and advice before the child has had the floor long enough to describe the real problem. In these first moments we parents are in danger of giving the wrong answer because our sons and daughters are often preoccupied with, "What does this conversation say about ME?" We parents thought the topic was the most important part!

> **Your child is listening to what the conversation says about him.**

To test the waters, a child-teen's first remark may be only a ticket of admission: "So, Mom, what's for supper?" This question may be just a version of "Can we talk?" Respond accordingly, keep your reaction short, give the airways back to your son or daughter quickly.

When they get around to the real subject, what should your first reaction be? If I were your child, I would hope that you would "hear me out," no early criticism, no quick attempt to fix blame.

The listening skills presented below may be familiar to you, but they are important enough for this reminder that we need them all.

Routines for talking and listening

Rule No. 1: Mind your body language.

Conversation is more than what is said and what is heard.

Before discussing what you say that sends the message, "I hear you," let's look at the *non*-verbal signals.

Maintain frequent eye contact. Remember that teacher who would never look at you? It was hard to pay attention in that class and almost impossible to ask a question. Of course, it's nerve-racking to have a person stare at you while you're talking, but a person who looks away too much says, "I have other interests."

> **Look at your child-teen, not continually, but frequently.**

For good eye contact, put aside the distracters that tell your child-teen you are not listening, the newspaper, the TV mute button, and computer mouse. Look at your child-teen, not continually, but frequently.

Face up to your listening responsibility. In order to listen to someone, you have to face them. It's obvious, I know, but often missed. It should be casual; there's no need to be "in their face" through the whole talk, but we all know the uncomfortable feeling of talking to someone who becomes distracted, turns away, or actually walks away while we struggle to keep up and finish our thought.

Along with facing him and keeping good eye contact, be aware of other postures that may send the wrong message. Slumping, stretching, and fidgeting all indicate a lack of attention.

Rule No. 2: Avoid instant personal criticism.

Your style of conversation sends a message about how you feel. Children are forever on guard to protect their fragile self-confidence. They are on the lookout for your evaluation of them as a person first; the topic of conversation, where we parents usually concentrate our efforts, is in second place, at best.

Your child may be totally preoccupied with extracting your personal evaluation during the first few sentences. If the signals are negative, up come the defensive reactions before any useful information comes out. If you hear your child say, "So what's your point?" or "What's your problem?" they may have learned you always have a problem or point. It might be time to change your reputation.

Mom: "So did you play nice with Kevin at his house?"
Josh: "Yes."
Mom: "You didn't fight with him."
Josh: "No, I didn't."
Mom: "Did you share?"
Josh: "Yes, can I go now?"

Mom's message here is that Josh may have been bad, and she wants to know so she can correct him. Josh has the message in the first question and wants to leave. Would Mom's reprimand of something that happened an hour or so ago be effective? Why is she searching for this possible mistake?

What happened over at Kevin's? Did Kevin do something that Josh needs to learn how to handle? Did anything unusual happen that Josh needs to have explained? We may never know; Mom has been busy reviewing Josh's conduct.

Mom's second attempt:
Mom: "Have a good time at Kevin's?"
Josh: "Yeah."
Mom: "What did you do?"
Josh: "Just watched TV."
Mom: "What? I didn't drive you over there to watch more TV!"

Until TV gets into it, Mom's second chance was going well, but the TV objection turns the whole conversation into instant argument. Josh didn't have complete control over what he and Kevin did. We don't know if watching TV was Josh's fault, but Mom's tone has him on the defensive. Mom may not like the activity (if watching TV is an activity), but bringing that into a conversation with Josh won't encourage him to say much more. With a third chance, Mom could go slower and listen more:

Mom: "TV?"
Josh: "Yeah, we got to fooling around and his sister fell off the couch."
Mom: "Fell?"
Josh: "Well, she was sort of pushed."
Mom: "Everybody has to be careful around little ones, Josh. Kevin knows that because he has his sister there all the time."

Her Mom held back criticism of TV and continued with neutral questions that didn't have "you" in them. When she heard of the roughhouse problem she started a little lecturing but she separated Josh from Josh's behavior, making it easier for him to talk about what happened, and allowing him to learn something. Let's give Dad a chance:

Adam: "You should have seen what happened in gym today, Dad."
Dad: "What, Adam?"
Adam: "Keith got into an argument with Mr. Effort and they ended up in a real fight!"
Dad: "I'm sure it wasn't much of a fight."
Adam: "Yes, it was! They were wrestling!"
Dad: "I hope you didn't have anything to do with it."
Adam: "Naw, all I did was cheer."
Dad: "Cheer? Listen Adam, you'll be in trouble right along with
Keith: "Don't you have any more sense than to…"

Let's interrupt Dad here just for a moment. Adam may resent the way his dad turned his story into a talk about the mistakes that Adam might have made. This experience will reduce his talks with Dad in the future. Dad criticized his son's story: (1) he thought Adam was wrong because it wasn't much of a fight; (2) Adam probably had something to do with it; and (3) he shouldn't have cheered. Dad centered the conversation on what he disliked about his son's behavior instead of the story. All in a 20-second discussion.

Remember the second rule of conversation is to avoid instant criticism. Let's back up and give Dad another chance to help Adam consider possible consequences of the gym-class experience.

Second chance:
Adam: "You should have seen what happened in gym today, Dad."
Dad: "What, Adam?"
Adam: "Keith got into an argument with Mr. Effort and they ended up in a real fight!"
Dad: "How did it all start?" (Dad ignores the possible exaggeration, doesn't express doubt, and shows interest instead.)
Adam: "They started arguing about the exercises, and Keith just wouldn't give in."
Dad: "Hard to win against the teacher." (Dad comments in general about the hopelessness of Keith's attitude instead of criticizing Adam.)
Adam: "Yeah. Keith is in big trouble."
Dad: "Did they ever get around to the exercises?" (Dad is interested in the story, not just in making points and giving advice.)
Adam: "Keith was sent to the office and then we tried these safety belts for the flips. Do you know about those?"
Dad: "I don't think we had them in my school."
Adam: "Well, you have these long ropes…"

Adam has a clearer view of the incident now, and he wasn't distracted with defending himself when he told the story to Dad. Now he's explaining something to his father, and Dad seems to think Adam has something interesting to say.

We all dislike instant evaluation, but young people are particularly self-centered and reactive to it. Some adults and almost all children fit into this category. Many family conversations go wrong because the child reacts to the early opinion expressed about him or her while we adults thought the topic was the most important part.

> We all dislike instant evaluation.

So your children may learn that all conversations with you are safe, because you seldom bring up their shortcomings and failures. Or they may learn you always have a criticism or advice to give and little talks with you should be avoided.

Rule No. 3: Take up the "It" instead of the "You" habit.

People who use positive communication are "easy to talk to." They seem interested in the other person (they talk about, and ask about, the other person). If conversation becomes threatening, they make it comfortable by using the third rule of conversation: they look at the problem as an "it" instead of something about you or me. In other words, they use neutral phrases such as, "it happened" or "what happened?" rather than, "What did *you* do?"

Mom: "How was art class today?"
Ethan: "Oh, OK, what I saw of it."
Mom: "What do you mean?"
Ethan: "Mrs. Clay sent me to the office."
Mom: "What did you do?"
Ethan: "I didn't do anything!"
Mom: "You must have done something; you aren't sent to the office for nothing!"
Ethan: (Taking up the "you" habit from Mom): "You never think it could be the teacher's fault: you always blame me!"
Mom: "What kind of talk is that? Let's have the whole story!"
Ethan: "Oh nuts!" (Ethan stomps out.)

This conversation goes wrong when Mom asks personal and threatening questions such as, "What do you mean?" and "What did you do?" All of this would have come out eventually, but her impatience erased any chance of helping Ethan. Mom could do better by keeping the personal threat at a low level and talking about the problem as an "it" topic instead of a "you" topic.

> **Mom could do better by treating the problem as an "it" topic.**

Second chance:
Mom: "How was art class today?"
Ethan: "Oh, OK, what I saw of it."
Mom: "You missed some of it?"
Ethan: "Mrs. Clay sent me to the office."
Mom: "What happened?" (Emphasizes the neutral word, "What" instead of "you." This is much better than "What did *you* do?")
Ethan: "Tom ripped my paper."
Mom: "Oh, no!" (Emphasizes sympathy rather than her child's upcoming mistake).
Ethan: "Yeah, so I shoved him."
Mom: "And so she sent you to the office?" (Emphasizes the punishment without adding to it.)
Ethan: "Yeah."
Mom: "Then what happened?"

Ethan: "Well, for one thing, I'm behind in art again."

Mom: "Well, if you can stay away from Tom maybe you'll catch up. What else happened today?" (Adds a little parental advice and then goes on to looking for something more positive to talk about.)

In the early years, kids can talk your ear off, but then somewhere in the preteens the mood starts to change. By the time she is 14, a daughter who is little Miss Yap-Yap in grade school can turn into Miss Sullen-and-Buried-in-her-Texting by high school.

Does the change have to do with hormones? I doubt it, because some normal kids never stop chattering and others even increase their habit of going on about nearly everything.

Even in the grade school years, the silent routine can become a habit depending on what they have learned to expect in family conversation. If your chances to find out what they're up to are rare, and your chances to tell them what to do are rare, you may have been meeting their expectations.

Too often we parents begin with the wrong end of the conversation. After our child or teen exposes a problem or troublesome topic, we often hurry to the end in order to fix a problem. In our rush, the message becomes, "Stop talking, you're wrong, I'm right, and I'll tell you what you should do."

> **Even a sassy teenager is not likely to have your way with words.**

Effective conversational strategies take more time, but if they become a habit, the rough parts of family talk can become smoother. Try these principles the next time family conversations and negotiations don't go well.

1. Deliberately slow your pace of conversation so your child-teen can slow his. Even a sassy teenager is not likely to have your way with words and will become defensive when he is rushed or runs out of vocabulary. Conversation doesn't make a good competitive sport.

Also, as mentioned before, kids are forever on the watch for "what does this conversation say about ME?" To accept your solution your teen has to stop thinking about himself and take up the courage to admit you could be right. Knowing how seldom your teen is likely to reach this opinion, start with step number 1—take your time. Most talks with your teen will not reach a conclusion. Let it end as it would with a friend at work—additional understanding, but no answers.

2. Watch the non-verbal signals. There is more to talking than what is said and heard. Folding arms, getting louder, and looking at the muted TV with your hand at the ready to restore the sound will irritate your son or daughter. A teen will quickly learn to increase aggressive behavior just to win back your attention. He responds to these body language cues but might not be aware of them.

3. Avoid jumping in with a "quick fix." Don't finish his sentence for him, the real subject may not have come up yet. If Mom or Dad jumps in too soon with advice, a teen may cancel his or her next topic entirely.

4. Identify and highlight the behaviors you like. Loving a child is not much without liking specific behaviors also. Mom and Dad's first parenting job is to find and compliment what is likable about their children. Even when their child feels obligated to brush them off. The compliments, not always recognized, will improve their self-respect. Repeat as needed. Learning is a process, not a single event.

5. Punishment is a last resort for the intolerable. It is likely to be imitated, and it is terrorizing when misunderstood. That makes it as inappropriate with children as it is with adults. If you show disapproval, they are likely to counter with why they are not wrong. When possible, it's better to point out the alternative behaviors that would have been better..

> Conversation doesn't make a good competitive sport.

Parental reactions that repeat what a teen just said often result in more information from the teen. His first remarks are usually long on feelings, short on facts, and may simply be intended to "test the waters" for your response.

Teen: "I've got so much homework."
Mom: "Sounds like…they gave you…a lot." (Good remark with the slow pace, and it only repeats what her teen said.)
Teen: "How can I do all of this?"
Mom: "Well, why not start with…" (Mom stops herself, remembers to avoid jumping in. Instead, she checks her body language.)
Teen: "I'm not going to do any of it!"
Mom: Starts to threaten grounding for a week if homework is not done, but remembers the five cautions on the next page and instead says, "You're really good at that math, maybe you could just start there." (Good compliment that risks a quick-fix mistake but, mixed with the compliment, it's likely to be taken positively.)

Keep a regular time and place for basic talking such as a long dinner time or, if possible, right after school as they get a snack. Don't try to fill every pause, some silence is OK. Don't meet their expectation that you always have (pushy) advice to give.

Five cautions: Beware the "quick fix" and the "games"

Caution No. 1: The real topic may not have come up yet.

Often a child's first remarks are only an expression of feelings without important details. If a parent reacts with advice and a "quick fix" right away, a child-teen may get derailed from his intended real topic.

In this situation, reflective statements are useful in order to hear the child out. The term, reflective, describes parental reactions that say nothing new, but simply repeat what the child said in different words. They send the message of "I heard what you said." They keep the conversation going without steering. Also, they provide opportunities to get straightforward information without defensiveness. Let's look at an example of reflective statements in action by a mother learning about her daughter.

Alanna: "Man, is that school boring!"
Mom: "It's really getting you down." (Mom just uses different words for "boring"; this is reflective and tells her daughter she is listening.)
Alanna: "You bet."
Mom: "What's getting so boring?" (Here's a good "it" question. It starts with "what" instead of "Why" (are *you* so bored?)
Alanna: "I don't know. I guess it's the whole thing."
Mom: "You need a break." (Good sympathetic remark that avoids, "There must be something wrong (with you).")
Alanna: "Yeah, but vacation is six weeks away."
Mom: "That's a long time. Got any plans?" (Good reflective statement that directs the conversation onto a positive topic.)
Alanna: "No."
Mom: "Hard to think that far ahead." (A reflective statement that merely repeats "no plans" in different words; it's also sympathetic and friendly.)
Alanna: "Pam is getting some applications for camps."
Mom: "Sounds like a good idea."
Alanna: "I might ask her about it."

A complaint about boredom such as this is familiar to most parents. Although not much is solved about boredom in this conversation, Mom has a better understanding of her daughter's feelings. Mom put the "quick fix" suggestion on hold and waited for the important topic to come up. Indirectly, Mom said she has had similar feelings to her daughter's and it's all right to have those feelings. Most important, it's all right to talk to Mom about feelings without being criticized for feeling "bored."

Because Mom allowed her daughter to direct the topic, information flowed to her. If she had directed the topic, information would have flowed from her as advice, but she would have learned very little about her daughter. Letting her daughter direct the conversation now gives Mom the added benefit of a "ticket of admission" to begin next time:

"Say, did Pam ever get any camp applications?" or,

"Only five weeks left now, how's it going?"

A few weeks and months of this effort from Mom and these two will be good friends. Notice Mom avoids old complaints in this approach. Frequent gripes such as, "You shouldn't be bored" and "You never plan ahead like Pam," are left out of the conversation. So are out-of-left-field complaints such as: "You never do your homework" and "You don't come when I call you." Such criticisms are too broad and, therefore, are likely to be taken personally because they say, "And while I'm thinking about you, another thing I don't like is…" Instead, Mom encouraged her daughter to take the conversational lead and parental complaints were postponed.

Caution No. 2: Arguments for entertainment's sake can be a habit.

Is the conversation just an argument for entertainment? The answer to this is particularly important when the argument is really about what your child says, not what she does. Intentions are not actions, but they can produce entertaining arguments. Your child may want a reaction from you or to convince you that you can't always control her. Some of your child's behavior in school or other places is away from your influence and that could be one reason school and other outside activities are her favorite topics.

A child's more obnoxious stories may be re-designed for your ears alone, just to push your button or get you to argue. Most of the time, your reaction should be plain vanilla, especially regarding abstract or distant situations.

When Todd's father first talked to me, he told me of Todd's stories about rude remarks he made to his teachers. The stories always resulted in a sharp reprimand from Dad.

Dad's typical reaction was: "You better watch what you say, those teachers work hard to help you and you just give them trouble!"

Then Todd would come back with: "Dad, you don't know, they

don't care about me, they're just in there for their paycheck!"

And Dad would counter with: "Well, you'd better listen to them if you want a paycheck of your own someday."

The argument is a destructive one, each looking for weaknesses in the other. No winners, no progress. But there is a little entertainment for Todd.

Todd said he didn't like these arguments, but that's questionable because he always came back for more. As a matter of fact, his mother told me, "I just don't get it. I think Todd deliberately stirs up his Dad."

Of course, Todd had no intention of insulting teachers. That was too dangerous. He just *talked* about insulting them, maybe to relieve frustration or to stir up a little excitement at home, or both. Being only ten, Todd might not even know he has a habit of putting down teachers at home, and no idea *at all* as to why he does it. If Todd's parents want a change, they need to work with the behavior in front of them, not the threat of what he does, or could do, at school.

> **Your reaction should be plain vanilla, especially regarding abstract or distant situations.**

We need new topics for Todd and his dad to talk about, and they need to be worked out in advance. If Dad has some good topics in mind, he and Todd won't be so easily drawn into new verbal fencing matches.

With new topics and Dad on the alert for chances to compliment and encourage Todd for reasonable conversation, the family airways will improve. Some of the best habits for parents are ones that help them stay alert to see and react to the best behavior of their children.

Reflecting a child's statements can help move her toward exploring alternatives and taking action to solve a problem. It helps when a parent sends messages that say, "I heard you" and "It's all right to feel the way you do." Then your daughter or son is likely to risk talking about possible answers to questions like: "What can I do about it?" or "What would help?" A parent helps most by tuning into the child's level of feeling and energy for the problem.

Is the child looking for alternatives, considering a particular one, or just venting emotion? All of these purposes are good. The parent must listen with empathy and react appropriately to give support. If the child is venting emotion, a helpful parent reflects that and does not give or push the child to look for answers.

Lori: "Mr. Factors is a terrible math teacher! He won't even let you ask a question."

Mom: "Questions are important in math—to get the problems straightened out before going on." Good. Mom stays clear of who is right, Lori or Mr. Factors.
Lori: "Sure. How can I learn if he won't answer the questions?"
Mom: "Does he ever review?"
Lori: "Oh, sure, he reviews, but it's so fast nobody knows what he's talking about."
Mom: "Why don't you go in after class?" (Whoops, Mom just took a superior view here. Lori may counter with, "That won't work" or "I tried that." Let's give Mom a second chance.)
Mom: "Why does he go so fast?"
Lori: "Who knows? What a jerk." (Lori's voice is lower now, running out of steam for this topic.)
Mom: "Some teachers are hard to deal with."

You may feel impatient with Mom in this conversation. Why doesn't she help? Couldn't she at least encourage Lori to go in after class? Or encourage her to speak up insistently in class?

If this is the third complaint about Mr. Factors, Mom might give some of that advice, but I think on the first round she should pass up the temptation to give advice and just let her daughter know she's on her side. How can her daughter feel comfortable and spontaneous in bringing up topics and venting some steam if Mom always makes the talk into a project to fix something?

Parents love to fix things, especially quickly! Parents, particularly fathers it seems, can be too efficiency-oriented in their conversations with kids. If you told me you had trouble tying your shoe because the lace broke, would you want me to tell you how to do it? No. As a matter of fact, it would be an insulting implication that you are a complete klutz!

So venting frustration is not necessarily a call for help. Remember, kids are always on the lookout for what the conversation says about them! An offer of help, especially too early, can be offensive because it's a message that says, "You don't know. Let me take over."

Here's another child, Kai, complaining for the fifth time about some obnoxious playmates. He's gone beyond the blowing-off-steam stage. The comment coming up is an indirect request for help. The reaction he gets from Mom is helpful in reviewing alternatives *he* suggests. If that doesn't work, and he asks for more help she will give her own advice.

Kai: "Those kids always bother me. I don't know what to do!"
Mom: "What *could* you do?"

Children are creative at listing options when they are ready. But if nothing comes up, the problem may not be clear yet, and he needs to explore more or just express more opinions and feelings. Perhaps he's ready to try an alternative.

Kai: "I'm going to tell those kids to quit bugging me!"
Mom: "How do you think they'll react to that?"
Kai: "They might stop, but if they don't I'll ignore them from now on."
Mom: "Just ignore them?"
Kai: "Yeah, that works every time!"

Well, it might not work every time, but at least Kai is in control and working on his own problem. Distinguishing different levels of emotion and energy and reacting with the right amount of support requires practice and empathy from a parent. When in doubt, be reflective and use it-questions, resist the temptation to suggest solutions.

Caution No. 3: Suggesting a solution may be offensive.

If you tell me you were late to work because of traffic and I say, "Next time you should avoid the main street and use the side streets." Are you likely to say, "What a great idea! I'll try that!" or is your reflex more likely to be, "I know all the side streets and I know the best way (mind your own business)"? You were just telling me how your day started, and I turned it into a driving lesson! From my side I may feel "I was just trying to help." But from your side it's offensive.

Our rush to fix problems comes partly from wanting to correct all the mistakes, but it also comes from viewing conversation as a game where every response on one side requires a "return volley." We all know people who see talking as a competitive sport—every action requires a reaction—preferably a "one-upmanship" answer. Among equals, the game might be tolerable, but children won't win very often and will probably learn to avoid games that they can't win.

So talking doesn't do very well as a competitive sport between you and your children—it's too one-sided. To avoid the game, someone will have to refrain from returning every challenge. Unlike tennis, you don't have to return every conversational ball served. So in addition to avoiding criticism by using "it" questions and reflective statements, we need to add another guideline: Use solution-suggesting statements carefully, only after all of the problem has been fully expressed. The purpose is to have the child explore for alternatives or just talk, not to have the parent suggest winning solutions. As an example, look at the temptations in the following conversation.

Maria: "Life is so depressing. People are so bad."

Mom: "I know it gets like that at times."

Here's a good start. It may seem like a terrible start because of the topic, but the topic is Maria's choice. A terrible start would be for Mom to fall to temptation and disagree right away by saying: "You shouldn't talk like that; there are a lot of good people in the world!"

Making this correction immediately would be tempting but it's unnecessary. Maria knows her remark is extreme. Also, it would be a little dishonest on Mom's part because she knows Maria is partly right. Since it's a statement with some potential for agreement, Mom takes the side that puts her closer to Maria. Let's see how it goes:

Maria: "It gets like that *all* the time at school."

Mom: "There must be some times that are good at school."

Not good. It's too early in the conversation for the implied disagreement, authority, and solution expressed in this nudge. Let's let Mom try again:

Mom: "School's been bad lately, huh?"

This is better because it's reflective, not argumentative, and without evaluation of who's to blame; it keeps the conversation focused on a third entity where Maria started it (not her fault; not Mom's). The next remark from Maria is likely to be informative about what the problem is at school. If Mom continues to "lay back," she will learn a great deal, and Terry will have the chance to "get it all out."

In most conversations between adults, the suggestions for solutions are *completely* left out. You don't often end a conversation with your neighbor, "So we're agreed you'll cut the hedge at least every two weeks," or "So don't go roaring off in your car like that, it disturbs everyone." With these reactions you would seldom see your neighbors!

Be satisfied that most conversations with your child, like those with your neighbor, will have little result. Leave out the closing comment, it risks turning the talk into a competitive game. If you try to be the "winner" in every talk, you will also make a "loser" each time. Frequent "losers" will soon call in absent.

Caution No. 4: They might not be ready to keep up with your speed.

Listening to a young child can be a frustrating experience. A son or daughter at three is pretty inefficient. Even when interrupting an older brother, talk can be an exasperating combination of demands and shortcomings:

Jessie: "Mom, I saw something outside, too!"
Mom: "Just a minute, let Damon finish."
Jessie: "But mine was really...ah...big, Mom, and, and..."
Mom: "OK, tell us what *you* saw."
Jessie: "Well, ummm, it was..."
Damon: "Dumb."
Mom: "Outside?"
Jessie: "Yeah, it was...a squirrel!"
Mom: "OK, OK, now let Damon finish."

Of course, your son or daughter knows it takes time to talk, and they struggle to keep up, to compete, and to hold attention. A parent's pace needs to be slower to take out the urgency and competition that causes so much of the trouble. While honing your listening skills, keep your pace under control in order for them to control their's.

Some of the pace, attitude and tolerance a child exhibits seems built in from the very start. Social styles differ—even in very young children—probably as a result of a constitution modified only a little by experience. Attempts to remake a child's social inclinations are likely to produce very little change and may only reinforce a child's feeling of isolation. Better to provide information and infrequent suggestions that allow a child to make his own way.

> **Keep your pace under control in order for them to control their's.**

One mom described the difference between her daughters this way: "Courtney and her sister Kelly are so different! Kelly can't stop talking and Courtney hardly says a word. It's hard to believe they were raised in the same family!

"Last week, I picked them up from a neighborhood birthday party and when I asked them how it went, Kelly said, 'It was great! They dropped all these balloons on us and everyone screamed! Samantha was there, A'isha was there, Cassie, and all the boys, Evan, Cole, Shawn, and Chris.'"

When Mom asked Courtney how it went she just said, "It was OK. Everyone was just running all over." Kelly said Courtney just stood around.

Being sociable is like many other activities: If you're good at it, you like it, and you tend to do more of it. On the other hand, if you don't get started with others easily, then you will have less practice with others and little chance of learning.

Kelly's focus is on others. She asks a lot of questions and

remembers a lot of details about what is going on. Courtney's concern is about her own security. She can't seem to think of anything safe to say. Both girls have habits that confirm their own expectations. Kelly talks a great deal, she is loud, and she has learned about the other children. Courtney doesn't talk much, uses a soft voice, and her lack of experience with the others leaves her short on subjects to bring up.

Courtney doesn't have a "problem." She has a quiet style which sometimes makes her feel left out. She shouldn't be given the extra burden of being told she has something wrong with her. But her parents could give her extra social ammunition when going into a social situation. Adults often help each other with this kind of priming: "Remember (Mom says on the way to her office party with Dad) my boss, Jessica, has that little boat out on the town lake, and she just got back from Florida. Her husband, Cole, bought a car just like ours, and Harold Teak's daughter just made him a grandfather."

These little bits of information will allow Dad to "go more than halfway" in starting a conversation with Mom's co-workers—if he wants to. Courtney needs help with information too. She may complain that "No one came over to me at the party." The parental reflex of "Did you go over to any of them?" could be left off while providing whatever information might be helpful to Courtney in thinking up something to start a conversation.

Dad doesn't get a lecture on how to correct some defect in himself on the way to Mom's party; he's just provided with a better chance of doing what he wants to do with information about the others. And Courtney doesn't need more criticism either, just some long-term help as the situations come up so that if she is inclined to join in the talk, the detail of thinking of a topic will be easier.

A child who is good at socializing has many friends; they agree with what she wants to do, laugh at the same things, and cooperate on the same tasks. They don't seem to try to please each other, they just do. The notion of being pleasing in order to get along with others may seem simple-minded and of little use until pleasing, agreeing, disagreeing, fighting and cooperating are seen as special cases of social rewards and punishments. Consider, for example, the following conversation I heard when visiting a first-grade art class. It took place at a table where three boys were working on pictures.

Justin: (Pokes Chris) "Don't do it like that, Dum Dum!"
Chris: "Leave me alone!"
Jon: "Give me the yellow."

Justin: (Reaches for the yellow crayon and pulls it close to himself) "I need it now."

Teacher: "Justin, give Jon the yellow crayon." (Justin throws the crayon at Jon and later Justin turns to Jon...)

Justin: "Are you through with the yellow now?"

Jon: "Yes."

As Jon starts to hand over the crayon, Justin grabs Jon's hand and digs out the crayon.

What are the special cases of reward and punishment during this art lesson? First, Justin punished Chris: "Don't do it like that, Dum-Dum." Second, Chris tried to punish Justin: "Leave me alone!" Third, Justin refused Jon's request for the crayon and later added another punishment by snatching it back when Jon offered it.

Justin was a punisher. He looked for things to punish, and if he didn't find them, he would punish good behaviors of others (Jon's offer of the crayon, for example). The best way to avoid punishment from Justin, perhaps the only way, is to avoid Justin!

Justin creates his own social world and probably finds that other children, and people in general, react negatively to him. To a great extent he controls his own world. He is a model of punishment for others and receives punishment from others who are copying him or just want to even the score.

> **Justin looked for things to punish, and if he didn't find them he would punish good behavior in others.**

For Justin to learn a new social style, someone will have to reward Justin for any acceptable response, and that person will have to be a good model as well. It's a tough assignment for a parent. The reflex reaction to such an unpleasant child is to react in kind, but Justin's mom will need to learn to watch for Justin's infrequent successes and coach his social style by encouraging the rare moments when he acts properly.

Justin's mother will also have to provide as little attention as possible when he punishes others. If he uses verbal abuse, she might try ignoring all but the worst of it. But remember that ignoring has to have the companion effort of "catch 'em being good!"

There is no quick fix to Justin's problem, and we'll have to settle for small successes in the midst of some not very pleasant situations. With close attention Justin's parents might find that certain situations are better than others. Justin's fatigue, hunger, or time when his parents are busy may indicate the worst moments, while family times after meals, but before

Justin is too tired, are the best times to look for good Justin-behavior to encourage. These good moments might be the most effective time for his parents to show a good example as well.

Caution No. 5: Children play odd games.

"Don't play games with me!" an aggravated parent will say. But everyone plays a few games and the first step toward dealing with them is made when the parent recognizes the game. The next step comes when Mom or Dad resolves to end it.

Game 1: "Referees are fun."

Travis: "Mom! Mark won't let me watch my program!"

Mom: "Mark, let your brother alone, Travis gets to watch his program now."

Mark: "It's a dumb program, and we can see the last of it later, I'm turning it to my show!"

Travis: "Mom! Mark changed the channel!"

Mom: "Mark, you come out here and help me and leave Travis alone!"

Travis: "Mom, Mark pushed me!"

Mark: "I have to get around you! Mom told me to go out there, so I have to push!"

Mom: "You two cut that out! Mark get out here right now! If I have to come in there..."

In this game, Mom is referee—the third party the kids go to for judgment calls, penalties, and control of the game. It's safer than regular conflict because they can count on Mom to call a halt to the escalation. By the way, as all Little League and soccer mothers know, referees are always 50 percent wrong. So if you lose, you can always blame the referee—what a comfortable way to pass the time!

Most referees are tempted to coach now and then. Parents are no different: "Mark, why don't you let Travis watch his program and then you can watch yours, and tomorrow at this time you will get to choose." Coach or arbitrator is more comfortable for a parent than referee. Referees give penalties and get blamed for everything wrong.

If Mom's solution is rejected, she could always end the game by removing the source of the argument—she could turn off the TV. The danger here is that one of the players may like that outcome. So calling off the game needs a promise that either side can have the TV for their half of the time by agreeing to Mom's solution. However, he still can't have his sibling's half.

The resolution here can't be perfect for the kids, but the goal is to get Mom out of the referee role. Many of these games become much less troublesome to parents when they identify the game and adjust their reactions to make sure they only play along when it's in everyone's best interest.

Game 2: "I'll bet you can't make me happy."

This game also pulls parents into the problems of their children when the children should be taking responsibility for themselves.

"Mom, what can I do, I'm bored."
"Why don't you work on your puzzle?"
"I've done everything but the sky part, and that's too hard."
"Well, how about helping me outside?"
"That's just work."
"Well, you might as well get your homework done."
"I don't have to do it yet."
"Well, why don't you..."

Many parents recognize this conversation as one that could go on and on. There's attention from Mom as long as no suggestion is right. As a matter of fact, if a suggestion were accepted, the game would be over. What would you do if old hard-headed Uncle Harry and his friend, Al, came over and started this game with you? You would probably make a few suggestions, and then since they are adults, you would think it was time for the old coots to entertain themselves.

Parents can't win the "I-bet-you-can't-make-me-happy" game. They just have to quit and let the children experience taking control of their own time.

Game 3: "My problem is your problem."

This is a common children's game that will develop later in teenage years into "It's your fault because you're my parent(s)." As with many of these games, frankly stating the fair truth may stop the game and allow some real progress.

"This homework is due tomorrow!"
"Well, you'd better get at it."
"Where's some paper?"
"In the desk."
"I already looked there."
"Why don't you try upstairs?"

"Mom! It's supposed to be down here! Could you go look?"

"Hold it, Lauren, your homework is your responsibility, not mine."

This game has a little of the flavor of the "I'll-bet-you-can't-make-me-happy" game. In both cases parental attention looks suspiciously like the reward that's prolonging the game, and it's time to put Lauren on her own for awhile to search for solutions.

Game 4: "You're the parent, let me tell you your job."

Troy: "I'd like to take those self-defense classes, Dad."
Dad: "Good exercise. And it could come in handy."
Troy: "Well, the ones I want to take are in Freetown."
Dad: "Freetown? That's almost an hour from here."
Troy: "Sam is in the one here and I don't like him."
Dad: "I can't drive two hours every Saturday because of Sam."
Troy: "You're supposed to help me, there's no other way."
Dad: "You could take the lessons here."
Troy: "You're the Dad, you're supposed to take me!"
Dad: "Troy, I'll be glad to take you to the lessons here, but I have a life on Saturdays, too. I'm not driving to Freetown."

Troy's game brings up the important notion that Dad has the right to be selfish at times. Troy's tactic of telling Dad what his responsibilities are isn't working, and he may change the game to:

Game 5: "If you serve me, I won't make you feel guilty."

Troy: "David's father drives him to Freetown."
Dad: "Well, I don't have that much time."
Troy: "Time for your own son?"
Dad: "Troy, don't start that. You know I spend a lot of time with you on our projects."

This isn't going well for Troy. If he doesn't think of a better argument, he's going to have to take lessons locally. Troy may have to start yet another game:

Game 6: "I'm not responsible; you are guilty for my mistakes."

Troy: "Well don't blame me if I get in a fight with Sam."
Dad: "What?"
Troy: "You're making me take the lessons here, so if I get into trouble it's your fault."
Dad: "Troy, You are responsible for what you do. If you and Sam can't get along, maybe you should skip the lessons."

Troy is almost out of ammunition for this argument and in

danger of having to show responsibility and consideration for Dad. He can't have his own way, and like the rest of us, he resents having to compromise and make an extra effort to get along. What tactic is left?

Game 7: "You're not right, because...because"

Troy: "Dad, it's not that far over there."
Dad: "It's the other side of the interstate!"
Troy: "The lessons here are not as good."
Dad: "You haven't tried any yet."
Troy: "They might cost more money here."
Dad: "Call and find out."

Is Troy going to agree now? Probably not. After asking Dad to make the call, bringing up Sam again, and getting out a map to show Dad he's wrong, he may call. Then, if Dad agrees on the price, he may start the lessons when he realizes Dad is not going to Freetown. The key here is Dad's firmness for his own welfare without attacking Troy with, "You're inconsiderate, irresponsible, selfish, etc." Dad sticks to the issues, not Troy's personal traits.

Game 8: "If you really loved me, you would serve me."

Here's a game that is similar to the "My-problem-is-your-problem" game with a little extra pull on the guilt strings of Dad or Mom.

"Mom, I need those shoes!"
"Jordan, I told you. You have a pair of running shoes—one pair is enough."
"But these are different. Ed's mom got him a pair."
"I said one pair is enough—it's too much money."
"Ed's mom said they're worth it for her son!"
"Jordan, don't run that guilt trip on me, I'm the one who bought you the first pair, remember?"

Calling Jordan on his attempt to blame Mom will not stop this argument, but when Mom recognizes the game, she has a better perspective and won't let her *son* get control of *her* emotions.

Good parental listening skills are crucial to handling the games that children play. If you have a tennis date with a player better than yourself, wouldn't it be nice if your opponent was a little distracted on the day of the match? You might be encouraged to try to put a few by her if only she were not paying attention. The same temptation can occur to a game-playing child when it seems Mom may be a little off her game or distracted.

When the game-playing conversation starts, look at your son or daughter rather than a TV screen or newspaper. To deal with a game you need all of your attention on it. Turn and face him or her so that there is no impression that you will miss what's really going on. These physical features of your attention let him or her know that you're not likely to be fooled by a game.

Feedback of what your child just said is a good habit during these conver- sations. Let him know that you heard what he said by repeating it. Avoid suggesting solutions in these games, they only lead to "make-me-happy" or "my-problem-is-yours." Also, suggesting solutions makes you sound superior and tempts your child to counter with something different just to stay even.

Take up the habit of asking questions in a form that is not threatening. Don't try to "win." Parents who frequently try to win by getting their son or daughter to *say* they'll try harder, be more responsible, or not be bad any more, may feel some progress has been made. But every time you're the winner and your child's the loser, the next conversation is likely to be more confrontational as your child tries to improve his record.

A good game tactic for parents is to "call 'em as they see 'em." "You know, I see you think I should take the blame for your mistake, but I really can't buy that." Or, "Look, Brian, I do love you, but you can't make every request of me a test. You need to handle this problem yourself."

EXERCISE:
Practice these listening skills and cautions in family conversation

With another parent or a friend, practice these listening skills and rules of conversation while you share a simple story such as a shopping trip, mild difficulty getting the kids to school, or helping them with homework. Begin with one person as the listener and one as the teller.

1. Keep eye contact. Look at your conversation partner most of the time. A child expects a good listener to look at him/her. We don't like to feel unattended because the person we're trying to talk to is staring at the newspaper or TV while we ask a question. Children feel that way too.

2. Use good posture. Face your son or daughter while talking and listening. Use body language that says, *"I'm alert! I'm interested!"* A

parent who slumps, looks away, or even *walks* away sends messages that discourage and insult the talker.

3. Avoid criticism and ask questions. Use questions that continue the conversation by asking for longer answers than just *"yes"* or *"no."* *"How did it feel?"* is more likely to continue the talk than "What time was it?" Emphasize IT questions instead of using YOU: "How was it at school today?" not "How did you do at school?" Careful questions asked in a neutral, non-opinionated way help the speaker discover a better understanding of what happened and why.

4. Avoid solution statements. Reword your partner's last statement to show you understand. *"Boy, I really hate that Mr. Jones for math!"* could be answered with, *"He really annoys you."* or *"You get mad in there a lot, I guess."*

5. Use reflective statements. Replace the temptation to give advice or criticism by reflecting your partner's statements instead. Suggestions such as *"Why don't you . . .?"* or *"Have you tried . . .?"* make the one with the problem feel inferior, resentful, and argumentative. You will get the whole story by reflecting, and your listening helps because the speaker will clarify the situation and his/her feelings by telling about it.

6. Share your experience. Share stories, jokes, and experiences that helped you learn about getting along in life. Be selective. Avoid stories that are too close to a sore point with your child. If your son or daughter feels your experiences are not directed as advice to his\her specific weaknesses, the tales can be enjoyed, and they will improve the relationship.

Chapter 2
Dealing with problems at home and at school

Everyone knows what pre-schoolers and grade-schoolers need to learn: eating, then sleeping through the night, then eating a variety of healthy foods and then getting along at school. At the early ages, the question is not what behaviors to teach but how to teach them. Four important principles can help parents teach effectively, keep their cool, and still have a happier day.

1. Emphasize the positive for preschoolers.

Look for the successes, not the failures. For example, in toilet training we parents are likely to focus on the mistakes, "Now look what you did. You have to use your words and tell me when you have to go!"

Although necessary, this approach, by itself, leads toward Mom being an angry person prone to criticism and punishment. Too much of this and the child could be intimidated from trying any communication, messy mistakes are likely to go up, and progress stops.

> **Look for the successes, not the failures.**

A focus on the successes, "Oh, thanks for telling me, that makes it so much easier. You're learning grown-up ways!" would tell the child more about what to do.

Opportunities to spotlight successes increase when a child is allowed to try out many solutions to her problem. Mom's problem is that her attention is easily drawn to mistakes—a disgusting accident or dirty diaper. Mom has to be alert for small successes. But one and half-year-olds have small vocabularies and few talking skills. So little Mary says, "Mommy, pick me up." not "Mommy, I need to go."

Mommy has to learn what Mary might mean by "pick me up" and she needs to "reward," that is, praise and encourage, Mary for finding a verbal signal even when it is not quite the right one. Diligence in looking for and encouraging the right behaviors when they happen, as well as discouraging mistakes is best. Positive reinforcement will encourage a person to be creative and explore many options. You can't make a garden by just pulling out the weeds.

2. Make a "Good Behaviors" list.

Most parents can easily list the bad behaviors they find objectionable but have only a vague idea of good behaviors they hope for. So "hitting his sister" may be high on the bad behaviors list.

Good behaviors such as saying something nice to your sister, talking in a normal tone, or petting the dog are often not specified at all. If Mom has nothing good to look for, she probably won't find it. Create a good behavior list, at least in your mind, pay attention to it, and compliment the successes.

3. Avoid the pitfalls of punishment.

Punishment doesn't teach much and it's likely to be imitated. Then everyone's behavior gets worse. Also, your reprimands may not have the negative effect you intend. There's always a challenging, maybe even entertaining, side if parents try to be too creative with negative reactions. Parents often suspect confrontations are, in part, entertainment. Keep your reprimands and time outs short and plain vanilla.

4. Like your children.

You love your children, of course, but do you like them? Do they know what you like about them? How do they know?

> Parents are about 100 percent successful in teaching the basics.

To be "cool," kids may ignore your compliments, but keep the positive feedback coming. It's a task worth remembering—often.

From toddlers and toilet training to teens and schoolwork, we are forever trying to teach our children. We start early with the basic three: eating, toilet training, and sleeping habits. Then we proceed to dressing, getting along with others, and on it goes. It follows that some teaching guidelines would help parents since they have to do so much of it.

Lucky for us, a lot of the teaching and learning comes naturally at first. And parents are about 100 percent successful in teaching the basics. You find few normal adults without good eating habits (perhaps too good) and very few adults without basic toilet, dressing, and sleeping habits. A parent can get anxious teaching these skills, but that usually comes from a self-imposed timetable placed in an already full schedule.

In the first stage, parents have little control over a baby's fidgeting, restlessness, hunger, fatigue, and need for an occasional diaper change, since these needs just happen to a child with little control by anyone. The basic three need special thoughtful reactions because the usual discouragements for mistakes and encouragements for successes have little impact on a baby.

As babies grow into toddlers and the basic three fade from their primary place in life, attention-getting behaviors develop. At this second stage, parents can more directly influence behavior because they are the source of attention.

Beyond the attention-getting stage (does it ever really end?), children develop additional needs for social and then school skills. Outside influences increase and, as they enter this third stage, many parents feel relegated to a coaching role on the sidelines of their child's life. Each stage requires more parental planning than the last so let's start with the basics.

Babies have simple needs and motivations without an extra or hidden agenda. That's why we treat the first two years as special. We don't blame the baby for crying, we assume he's hungry, sleepy, or uncomfortable. We all know babies are innocent and their understanding of the world starts at nearly zero. Parents hope to build communication quickly and work at it all the time. They also look for signs of successful communication and marvel at the discoveries of progress. The successes of an infant are a source of satisfaction and one of the greatest joys of parenting.

"Dawn slept through the night almost from the very beginning."

"Jeremy was walking by the time he was one!"

Our ambitions for our children can make us proud of whatever they accomplish, but can also lead us to exaggerations because we want to see progress so badly. And we look for any progress in understanding so our job will become easier.

"It was obvious Terry knew right from wrong even before she could talk!"

"She understands 'No!' just fine; she's just ignoring me."

Exaggerations in the areas of understanding and communication can be dangerous. They can lead parents to rules that are only confusing to the child and frustrating to the parents.

For the first two years, most behavior needs to be influenced directly without the use of consequences for learning. For example, careful parents put dangerous items out of harm's way—not "letting her find out for herself" that pulling on a wobbly chair is dangerous or that a sharp knife cuts. We can't afford to let him "deal with it" or "follow his own instincts."

Personality development during these first years comes mostly from physical changes and lots of loving stimulation by parents. Learning of the complex kind comes later. For newborns, stimulation by holding, cuddling, and talking will do more than provide comfort, it will "exercise" the brain and contribute to development. Needs should be met quickly. "Crying it out" makes no sense to a baby who barely knows what's the matter, let alone what "being patient" is all about.

For toddlers, parents need to do a lot more "environmental engineering," removing and putting out of sight all dangerous and fragile objects. That will be a lot easier than trying to teach a child the difference between glass and plastic when he has yet to learn the difference between food and dirt!

Parents of toddlers should be extra careful to separate *the child* from *the action* in both their own minds and in their corrections of the child. Blame is already a sensitive topic. For children under two, even time-outs are not effective. As an alternative, parents could remove the offending child from the situation and stay with him or her for a few seconds. The interruption can give both child and parent a fresh start.

The basic three

Sleeping, eating, and toilet training—are in troublesome territory. Parents have limited control and little information about the real moment-to-moment needs of their child along with a strong desire for everything to go well for their child's health. The three are such natural and necessary behaviors you would think they would be the easiest for parents to teach and children to learn.

Since almost all adults end up learning the basic three, we know the job is eventually accomplished. Why is it, then, that the basic three are often the *basic troubles* for parents? As all experienced parents know, emotions about the basics get in the way. Eating, sleeping, and elimination have special characteristics beyond just getting energy, rest, and essentials for health.

Keep these six aspects of the basic three in mind.

1. The basic three are somewhat out of the control of parents. You can't directly force someone to eat, sleep, or use the bathroom.

2. The only direct information about the moment-to-moment needs for food, sleep, or elimination comes from the child and is not directly observable by parents.

3. The behaviors are somewhat out of the control of the child as well. Other conditions, deprivations, and feelings enter in. A child cannot feel hungry on demand or sleep any time the request comes up.

4. The basic three are partly driven by even more obscure conditions, experiences, and habits that may seem irrelevant. Even with us adults, our eating, sleeping, and bathroom activities are related, in a way not completely understood, to coffee, tea, excitement, boredom, depression, worries and fears, too little or too much exercise, or the need to escape an unpleasant situation—just to name a few.

5. Cultural taboos are emphasized in the basic three. Mistakes here produce the most wrath, embarrassment, and guilt. Under that pressure, children learning the basic three are somewhat at the mercy of the conditions mentioned above and yet squeezed by the emotional pressures.

Parents can help by controlling daily experiences, diet, and deprivations, but rules with consequences must be handled carefully. It is tempting to make demands on children who are too young. With children who may not be developed enough to perform, the risks of mistakes, disappointments, and lasting confrontations are very high.

6. Being private activities, the basic three also comprise the last bastion of control and privacy of one's own life. They are the last places any one of us, child or adult, is likely to tolerate interference. For example, one theory of anorexia (refusal to eat) is that the person needs to protect some control over at least part of her life. As one daughter said to me, "They (parents, relatives, teachers, and nearly everyone else) tell me what to wear, when to wear it, when to get up, play, do homework, and go to bed. But they can't *make* me eat. At least I control that! And I'll prove it, I won't eat anything!"

Eating.

Children can eat or not eat for fun, adventure, attention, "control" of the situation, or to "win" in a power struggle with Mom or Dad. For the most common family situations, a parent's strongest strategy is just engineering the environment.

The fundamental strategy is similar to the same limits we have for adults in the household. Eating is limited to what is in the house and provided at the table, leaving the choices as much as possible to the person. *Your best time for tough diet decisions, the time when you have the most control, is when you are shopping for food.* Postponing the decision by bringing cookies and cake home and then delaying or denying them to the kids only opens the door for long arguments.

It's better to take control where you have it, at the supermarket. Instead of bringing home a gallon of ice cream and then practically needing a refrigerator lock or dog-leash to keep the kids from eating it, you're better off buying only a small amount or not buying it at all. Left with the selection you provide and their own judgment, most children will select a good diet overall with a few mistakes.

Outside the home they will also make plenty of mistakes, deviating from what is good for them along the way—the same pattern you find in us adults. To emphasize this area of behavior when no serious problem exists treads on dangerous territory for no good reason.

Many families report that their mealtimes highlight their biggest complaints. The atmosphere there extends into the other family activities. So any extra unjustified confrontation is not in the best interest of the family. If you are going to use a tougher rule about eating, be sure the goal is worth the effort and that the performance required is well within range of your daughter's (or son's) abilities.

Maybe the rule (to eat *all* food served) is too big a step and one not even required of adults. Possibly we need an easier rule with the choices limited by what is available.

You could decide that your daughter can't have dessert until she has finished the food on her plate, but this might be ineffective if she is allowed snacks later while watching TV. But allowing alternative freebies is no sin unless it weakens the usefulness of an important rule. You might remove these alternative freebies and find that your daughter still doesn't care about the dessert option.

Look carefully at the rule and the level of performance it requires. The goal is for the child to recognize and satisfy his or her own hunger with what's available. If parental demands and arguments insist on too much control, the child may ignore his own body cues of hunger while starting arguments and power struggles instead; then the stage is set for trouble.

Sleeping.

Sleeping problems can be a whole different level of anxiety for parents. While many adults hold easily to a sleeping pattern, it is usually an individual pattern with frequent variations from week to week.

A child deserves the same flexibility. Painful as it may be after a full day of demanding parenting, the fact is that a child's need for sleep is still a product of many variables. However, if bed, bedtime, and isolation in the bedroom have not been used for punishment during the day, sleeping will be welcomed at least as often as it is for adults. The cautions on using sleeping, naps, and isolation in bed as a time-out are discussed in Chapter 6. Usually the price to be paid at bedtime is too high for a comfortable family situation.

A child's unpredictable bedtime behavior may be a problem only in the mind of the parent and then developed from the parental reactions *into* a larger problem. Better to look first at the diet and exercise. Snacks with caffeine, such as a glass of soda or chocolate milk, can disturb the sleep of a 150-pound adult; think how concentrated that amount is in a small child!

> **Determining what plays a role in your child's sleep pattern is your best hope for progress.**

Perhaps a behavior chart from the exercise on page 67 is in order here. Drinks, particularly those with sugar or, please forbid it, caffeine, should be recorded in the behavior chart along with time of day, other food, the day's exercise, naps, and the discussion of problems and worries in the evening. Also add a place on the page for TV, both amount and type. Determining which of these activities plays a role in your child's sleep pattern is your best hope for progress.

Since sleep problems can be influenced by exercise and naps during the day, the behavior chart on sleep should include these activities also. So the first point is not to approach the problem as if it could be influenced by consequences at bedtime but rather to approach it as if it could be influenced, as it is with adults, by the day already done. Also, it's important to establish a pleasant routine of bathing and reading. Let the time of the routine vary as needed.

Toilet Training.

Most psychologists consider toilet training a crucial childhood experience. Theories back to Freud, and before him, have discussed the symbolic nature of the behavior. In the practical situation, toilet training acquires some of its importance from the natural reaction of parents to the disgusting outcomes of mistakes. The emotions are first in the mind of the parent and not yet the child.

Be comforted by the fact that nearly everyone arrives at adulthood having learned this talent despite all the parental concern and anxiety. Very few children make it to four without great progress in this area. Mistakes occur even with teenagers when the "child" is distracted or excited, but regardless of the method, we parents have about 100 percent success in this area—not something we can say about all the projects in this book!

Most children can begin toilet training between two and four. Starting toilet training too soon will produce the most mistakes and disappointments because the parent cannot control this behavior and it may not yet be controllable by the child. An early start also risks bigger problems and confrontations later.

The mistakes produce the emotion, so it would be best to maximize the possibilities of rewards for success. First you need a "behavior chart" to put by the diaper pail. Write in the hours of the day across the top and note every time a diaper goes into the pail. Label a row for each day and leave a space for "remarks."

The use of 1's and 2's for wet and dirty diapers can give you some notion of when the best time for training would be. When the numbers collect at certain times of the day, you have an indication of when training is likely to be successful. If "accidents" are still happening at all times of the day, it's not time to start.

When the training starts, continue your chart to note successes and rewards. The best reward will be your reaction, but you may want to include a treat for success. At first you'll need to give encouragement just for staying on the toilet. Later, the rewards can come for successes.

If there has already been some emotion over this training and your child is resisting, you may need to start with a potty chair in a new situation and gradually move the training back to the bathroom. For example, you might begin by rewarding your child for sitting on a portable potty in another room, then the hall, then into the bathroom. Keep the praise up, the emotion down, and the tolerance high. Remember that all the adults you know eventually learned this, and you don't have to meet anybody's schedule.

Occasional bed-wetting is not unusual for children under the age of 10. Lined underpants or big-child diapers may have to serve as a temporary solution. Frequent bed-wetting can be a medical problem because certain infections of the bladder and urinary tract produce uncontrolled urination.

The first place to start on this problem is at your physician's office. When you are sure that a physical ailment is not the problem, you could use a bed-wetting alert device that consists of special pants with a lining that detects moisture and sets off a buzzer similar to a loud alarm clock. Since bed-wetting does not begin abruptly, the child has time to wake up and go to the bathroom when the buzzer sounds.

Over a few weeks this battery-operated alarm clock for bed-wetting can teach a child to wake up and use the bathroom. One source for the device is Sears Home Healthcare catalog. Similar devices are clipped into a standard disposable panty-liner which is attached to a credit-card-size beeper unit worn on the child's shoulder. These are available from Dri-Sleeper (www.dri-sleeper.com) or Potty Pager (Ideas for Living) 1285 N. Cedarbrook, Boulder, CO 80304.

For more sources, look up "Bed-Wetting Control Systems" on the Internet.

Parents must get up with the bed-wetting alarm, too. As with most child-rearing problems, a gadget by itself will not solve the problem. You may have to help the child shake out the cobwebs to be awake enough to even find the bathroom! A little support for a job well done and you're back to bed without a big event.

The effort is worth it because bed-wetting can complicate other difficulties—fears of sleeping, staying overnight with relatives or friends, embarrassment, and shyness.

Challenges of attention-getting behavior

Parents usually suspect that some of a child's bad behavior occurs because of the attention it attracts, and their first question should be, "Why can't my child get the attention he or she needs some other way?"

Some children may only receive attention and consideration from the family when they act up. Other children may have developed more pleasing solutions to their attention-getting problem, but if the overall amount of attention drops, they will resort to bad behavior to make up the shortfall. If this strategy works, we might call the child "spoiled."

A "spoiled" child has found a way to control his parents' behavior by punishing them with bad behavior or the threat of it. "Spoiled" is a catch-all term describing many behaviors, some of which may not be bad. The behavior a child uses is often embarrassing, exasperating, or just plain annoying to the parents. He uses it because it works.

> **A child uses bad behavior because it works.**

The way out of the problem lies in the direction of rewarding the little good behavior there is in a child who may not seem very likable or deserving. Added to the "catch 'em being good" rule should be an extinction rule for obnoxious behavior.

Extinction refers to a rule about withholding consequences. In this case, it would be withholding attention and not giving in to obnoxious behavior. Single out one aspect of the "spoiled" behavior and write up an extinction rule about it. For example, if the child begins to fuss when he is about to be deprived of something, eliminate the possibility of any change in that decision.

Notice the rule in this case singles out fussing and does not include any other part of what is called being "spoiled." Angry, pouting, and other obnoxious behaviors are not part of this rule. For these other behaviors you'll just go with your on-the-spot reactions, dealing with mistakes as the situation requires. That on-the-spot decision may include holding to the decision that produced the bad behavior, but the fussing rule that says fussing is *always* ineffective in getting a parental reversal still remains.

> **If obnoxious behavior is "required," then obnoxious behavior will be learned.**

The reason for this separation of strategies is that an extinction rule is hard to follow. If it is too broad, it will force you to look for too many behaviors at once and consistency will suffer. The small separate rule is more likely to encourage you because any change in the bad behavior highlighted in the rule, in this case, fussing, will stand out as a success. Knowing that the extinction rule really works, you have a better chance of holding to the rule in another situation.

Remember a "spoiled" child did not get that way because too much was provided. Many children in families with small incomes are "spoiled," and many children with the benefits of wealthy families are not "spoiled." The parent's routine reactions to a child's demands determine a child's habit. If obnoxious behavior is "required," then obnoxious behavior will be learned.

Some parents have told me that they avoided giving in to bad behavior but ended up with a problem child nevertheless. I think many of these parents did, occasionally, avoid supporting bad behavior, but even infrequent giving in can encourage bad behavior.

If parents ignore bad behavior but don't send a clear message about what is *right*, a child casts around for solutions to his needs and frustrations. What will he find that works? Over the months and years of growing from a one-year-old to a ten-year-old he will develop his own theory of how to handle these low moments. It may be acting "spoiled," "angry," or "nice." Without much feedback from a specific plan and effort to support good behavior, a child needs only a few accidental and unfortunate experiences to become troublesome.

Fussing, dropping, and throwing

These are behaviors that have many things in common. They are directed at the parents. They are often maintained by attention from the parents—justified or unjustified. And they go away as the child grows up or at least they are replaced by more "adult" manipulations for attracting attention.

Your kitchen chart can come in handy for these behaviors. Keep a record of when the problem occurs. What happened right before and right after the outburst? You may already know that part of the fussing is a result of fatigue late in the day or before nap-time. But the fussing may also come up for, or be used on, certain members of the family—Mom gets the fussing, Dad gets the pouting, for example. Now a little examination of what often happens *next* and a possible change may become obvious. Dad needs to watch his reactions to pouting—even teasing about it may be a reward.

Mom and Dad also need to watch how their child plays Mom and Dad against each other. A particular circumstance or time of day may make a child's bad behavior or a parent's mistakes more likely.

Many parents find that saying, "Please use your words, not the fussing," helps a fussing child get back on track.

For the dropping and throwing part of attention-getting, we need to emphasize reactions to good behaviors and as little reaction as possible to bad ones. We also may need a "Count-out or Time-out" rule as described on page 202.

Behavior during illness.

Every parent knows that a sick child produces the most upsetting and helpless feelings in parenthood. This situation changes all the rules. The child needs special attention and so do the ground rules of the family. Everyone wants to make the patient comfortable. With children, particularly, the unusual nature of the situation has to be emphasized because there are dangers here for long-term effects from the illness experience.

We don't want her to learn that special advantages are available whenever she *says* she is ill. This has the potential to be one of those unfortunate experiences that shape bad social habits in the future. References to illness are not always verifiable—a headache or upset stomach is a hard claim to check out. Even the child may not be aware that he is exaggerating and using certain claims to control attention from his parents.

Again, positively stated rules that allow parents to love and attend their child for good reasons are a part of the solution. Also, some of the less attractive but logical consequences of being ill might be emphasized whenever there is reason for suspicion. For example, if a child claims to have a headache and so wants to watch television instead of doing homework, perhaps your first response should be that he lie down and take a nap instead.

Reasonable suggestions should become consistent and prompt reactions to a child beginning to use illness for its secondary benefits. If a child says he has a headache, it is probably best to act as if he does. A long argument about whether or not he *really* has a headache only increases the probability that we might be giving attention for bad behavior. But having a headache shouldn't mean all demands are off and the child gets to do whatever he or she wants. It should mean acting reasonably to reduce the headache—rest, quiet, and eating only sensible food.

If you are wondering if illnesses are real, set up a chart similar to that described for fussing. A week's record might show up some regularities to help sort out illness from fakery.

The "Linus" syndrome of thumb and blanket.

Thumb-sucking or the use of a comforter such as a favorite blanket, serves the need for security but can also develop into an attention-getting device. Parents who feel the habit has gone on too long should remember that we all give up our special comforter eventually. So the question is whether or not to hurry the process along.

A little soul-searching can determine whether the problem is with the child or in the mind of the parent. Sometimes parents will say, "It just bothers me that he(she) is still doing that." If the problem is only in the mind of the beholder, perhaps it should be dealt with there.

Breaking the thumb and/or blanket habit is a stressful process at best and may be downright traumatic. If something is to be done, the emphasis ought to be on positive support for activities that require ignoring the blanket and thumb for a while. Improvement without new emotional problems is almost impossible if discouragement and reprimands for using the comforter are frequent.

Usually the child will latch on to some new way of dealing with stress, either choosing to be alone more often or using a defense tactic such as crying, pouting, or throwing tantrums until assured that everything is again under (the child's) control.

Tantrums.

When a child who occasionally throws tantrums requests something, parents need to make a careful decision. As every parent knows, the decision to deny the request should not be altered by a tantrum, but often a less clear reaction gets parents into hotter water. The request from an explosive child may tempt the parents to put off a confrontation with, "I'll think about it," or "We'll have to wait until your mother (or father) comes home." This sets up a long and risky period when a tantrum is likely. For the moment the request has been denied, but it was done in a weak way that tempts the child to fight for what he or she wants—plenty of time to try out a tantrum along with other obnoxious behavior.

Also, putting off the child leaves him with nothing to do for the moment. It takes experience and creativity to put aside one line of activity and take up another while waiting for an answer to come down from the parental powers. Instead of switching to a new activity, the *childish* thing to do is cling to the present direction and push for closure. Nagging is followed by complaining, then frustration and attack, and then the whole tantrum.

> **The decision to deny a request should not be altered by a tantrum.**

Another argument for prompt decisions is that they allow less time for a tantrum to develop and for parents to give in. With longer delays, it's tempting to hold out until bad behavior gets worse, then giving in is certainly a move in the wrong direction. Delays in decisions and giving in to expanding tantrums develop the childish willingness to try to manipulate others by making them miserable.

Unreasonable fears.

One of the major difficulties in dealing with unreasonable fears in children is the parental suspicion that the child is exaggerating for effect.

Fears first developed from scary experiences can be accidentally encouraged with too much attention. By maintaining the fear with extra attention and accommodation, we now have a whole new additional problem. What at first was motivated by love and was an acceptable way of helping a child through some difficult and scary circumstances can become a parental routine that now maintains unwanted behavior.

Of course the fears also exist within the child and they deserve our sympathetic understanding. So while a parent is sleeping with a frightened child, sitting with one who is afraid of the dark, or carrying a child who is afraid of dogs, a gradual reduction of these accommodations to a reasonable level needs to be in the plan. But an abrupt, cold turkey approach is not in order.

Dragging a kicking and screaming child up to a dog in an effort to "get him to understand" that most dogs are nice, only makes him fear you as well as dogs!

Remember that fears are expressed as behaviors but are not necessarily rational. Rationality (*talking* them out of it) will not be very effective. Many fears are conditioned reactions from past traumatic experiences, and this conditioning is not a rational process.

If Pavlov's dogs had been rational about conditioning, they would have ignored the bell and saved their spit until the food arrived! Their irrational reaction (salivation) to the bell was not done *in order to* get the result they wanted (food). Salivation just happened because the food was *always* presented after the bell. So even if Pavlov's dogs could understand, they would not have been talked out of sloppy anticipation.

Conditioning, being more reflex than purposeful, will not yield to argument.

So neither arguments nor the sink-or-swim technique is likely to produce a cure. The problem calls for a gradual change in the *situation*. For example, fear of the dark will have to start with a light which is gradually dimmer or placed farther away. This kind of fading procedure over weeks coupled with lots of support and compliments for small successes can reduce the problem to leaving only a night-light or small table light on.

Strategies require effort. So the first question to ask about a troublesome fear is whether or not the problem is serious enough to require attention—any attention. If not, then your reactions should be carefully selected to show the appropriate loving sympathy with no additional attention or consequence.

Most childhood fears fade away naturally as the result of varying degrees of contact with the feared situation. Parents should keep in mind that time and understanding are great healers, *if* there is no attention-getting aspect in the parents' reaction to maintain the fear.

Compulsions and fidget behavior.

Nail-biting, hair-twirling, nose-picking, and lip-biting are usually maintained partly by parental attention and partly by the absence of something else to do. They are behaviors that fill up time and are occasionally rewarded accidentally by parents.

However, fidget behavior can be more complicated than plain fidgeting. It's fidgeting with a long-term commitment. It happens in the slow, somewhat boring moments of life and almost everyone does it. At first it can be just the random squirming and wiggling of a child.

To a child we say, "Stop that fidgeting!" Later on, the little habits develop into hair-twirling, scratching, or ballpoint pen-clicking (for us older ones). Even eating and drinking can develop into fidget (fill-up-the-dull-time) behaviors. A well-known psychology experiment concerning fidget behavior has been repeated many times with both people and animals. In one example, a laboratory white rat is trained to press a lever for food. He soon learns that the food is only given for lever presses after long intervals—about two minutes. In the meantime there is little to do but wait. What to do, what to do? A water bottle is available, but the rat has water all the time in his home cage so he is not thirsty. But, faced with nothing to do, he drinks (remind you of anyone?).

It is not in the rat's nature, or ours, to do absolutely nothing. With humans, doing nothing is even embarrassing. So we pretend to read (or something) in waiting rooms, in restaurants, and airports. Many of us wouldn't go to a restaurant alone without something to read.

So the rat drinks. But he does not just sip! He may drink up to two times his body weight in water while waiting for the intervals to pass! Since no rat has a bladder that big, you can see that the experiment requires regular cleaning chores.

All that was needed to stop our furry waterholic was to shorten the waiting time—down from 2 minutes to 30 seconds. With the shorter interval all the excess water-drinking was gone. Pay-offs came more often, there was work to be done, and our rat had no time for fooling around!

So now we have *two* possible explanations of frequent, repeated, annoying behaviors. One, they could be fidget behaviors to pass the time and, two, they could be attention-getting. The difference is important.

For attention-getting behaviors we need a strategy that reduces the attention for that behavior. For fidget behaviors we need to also reduce the boredom, the down time, the dull moments. Take a little extra time for reflection when you first see the beginnings of a "nervous" habit or a "compulsive" behavior.

> **Nail-biting, hair-twirling, and other fidget behaviors fill up time and are occasionally rewarded accidentally by parental attention.**

Rewarding other, more desirable behaviors will be a good strategy in either case, but the reaction to the annoying behavior itself should be a careful one. For attention-getting activities you certainly want to reduce attention, but for a fidget behavior, there is all the more reason to see that support and opportunity for more acceptable behavior occur more often.

"Jumping on" fidgeting behavior can be a dangerous parental habit. If the bad behavior thrives on attention, a parent will need a long remedial strategy later. If the behavior is not important, let's not make it so. Instead let's look to the situation for a way of enriching the moments.

Any smoker or heavy drinker will recognize the fidgeting aspect of their habit and tell you that the worst time of temptation is during the low moments—not just the depressing ones, but the boring ones, also.

Another strategy for fidget habits is to reward the lack of compulsive behavior. For example, one mother told me she promised a dollar to her son if he could refrain from nail-biting long enough so that his nails would need cutting. Because this demand seemed a bit too large for a first step, her son was also given a quarter for each one of his fingernails that needed trimming because it had been allowed to grow.

Such a direct rule about a compulsive behavior must be used carefully. There is always a tendency to do more than just state the rule, and nagging ensures that attention will be connected to mistakes.

As with any attention-getting behavior, in the child's view she is not getting enough attention and found a behavior that seems to alleviate the deprivation. If we now come along with a new strategy that sees to it that the child's solution for getting attention will not work, then we need to look for a new behavior for the child that will work. That new way to appropriate attention should be one the child can easily accomplish.

Rhythmic habits.

Although rhythmic habits are sometimes symptoms of severe childhood disorders, normal children and adults have rhythmic habits, too. Tapping a pencil, swinging a foot, and rocking to music may annoy parents but are probably too trivial to merit a strategy beyond ignoring.

When a habit grows and becomes troublesome, most parents can remember its beginning as a less frequent event. This can be a case of parents trying to fix a non-problem and now they have a problem.

A behavior that started as just fidgeting became a gimmick for attention, and then a way to express exasperation at the parents. "Getting through to" the parents now produces a reprimand, a new kind of attention in a situation where positive attention seems unlikely to the child.

An occasional correction or request to stop the annoying habit is not likely to do much harm if the parent's emotional reaction can be kept in check.

Consider this situation. Aaron has been banging his foot on the chair leg at dinner for three minutes.

Mom: "Aaron, stop kicking the chair—it's a bother when we're eating."
Aaron: "I can't help it."
Mom: (Still in a very quiet tone.) "Well if you can't help it, you'll have to eat in the small chair with your feet on the floor. Did you finish your picture before dinner?"
Aaron: (Still kicking the chair.) "Yes, it's a boat."
Mom: "A boat. I'd like to see it after we're finished. Please don't kick."
Aaron: "I told you I can't help it."
Mom: (Still very calmly) "If you continue, you'll have to be in the little chair. That's one." The count-out begins.

Aaron may have to go to three and then to the little chair a few more times. Later, if his kicking ploy to get Mom going doesn't work, he'll stop or at least keep his excess energy habits at a tolerable level. Mom is right to provide another direction for Aaron's focus. These other topics will have to become a regular part of Mom's habits *before* the chair kicking or other problem starts. If Mom only comes up with these interests when Aaron acts up, you can see where that will lead.

Taking all that "flak."

One obvious characteristic of a child's bad behavior is that it generally reduces the demands from his parents. Parents can silence a child or keep him from acting up by taking a threatening pose that implies punishment. And, of course, *the child* learns and uses the same idea, but since he is a less powerful figure he must use it in a more subtle way.

The child's threats and lack of compliance make up his version of "flak," some parents will give in rather than "take all that flak."

Cindy uses flak to put her mother off and to avoid some requests for work. But Cindy's behavior is also a result of the fact that the request is *just* work. There's no payoff for her.

By this time you may be getting a little tired of the idea that everything has to pay off, but remember that what we mean by "pay off" in many cases is just the honest adult expression of appreciation, admiration, or support for something good or helpful.

Material reward is not always necessary. In your job you probably do many things because you have come to believe that it is the right way to do it or that it will please someone. You don't necessarily do it just for the money.

> **Pay off in many cases is just the honest adult expression of appreciation, admiration, or support.**

Why don't you try flak with your boss? Because it won't work, I would bet. And also with a good boss, it never occurred to you to give her any flak because there is consistent support for doing the job—satisfaction and appreciation as well as pay.

Cindy's parents try to bring about some effort from Cindy by coercion and Cindy avoids that effort, if she can, because it is straight coercion without a significant parental reaction.

When Cindy is using flak, she often exposes the situation quite well by saying, "Oh, why should I do that anyway?" The statement is pure flak intended to stop a request from Mom or Dad, but, incidentally, it asks a very good question: "What does Cindy get out of it?"

Although it is easy to attempt to coerce behavior, it is usually ineffective. Better to plan and provide support for a variety of chores. Plan reasonable, positive consequences and opportunities for more social approval to open the way for more willing help next time.

The challenge of a child becoming a student

"Mom (Dad), how will I make the grade?"

Comfort and success in school are crucial ingredients in the happiness of children and their parents. The way to this success goes beyond just feeling pride in learning basic skills. In the first few grades, the most important development is a child's self-confidence and positive expectation for what school has to offer.

If you can help your child to be comfortable and positive about school, what a gift it is! And that success not only builds confidence in academic abili-ties, it influences feelings of competence and usefulness outside of school as well.

Parents of children-turned-students have a new job beyond helping with homework. Parental advice for good school skills and efforts to use the learning at home will boost the child's confidence and attitude.

Your first years in school helped shape your early definition of who you were. Comparisons with schoolmates fixed your impression of them and shaped a judgment of yourself as well, all before you were ten, no doubt. Parents who have attended their own school reunion know how the reunion seems to measure us against that old bench-mark again. This common reaction to reunions demonstrates how durable help in school is to a child.

We all know the first school days are a big adjustment for a child, but they are also a big adjustment for parents. It is probably the first time parents are required to share their:

1. Child-rearing attitudes,
2. Influence through reinforcement,
3. Control of what will be learned, and
4. Control of the daily schedule.

Sharing means that other people become important to the child. The strategies and habits a child learned for dealing with parents might not fit the new people and the new situation.

Greg: "Mom, I don't want to go to school any more."

Mom: "What? I thought you liked school."

Greg: "Well, it's boring and the kids don't like me."

Mom: "Getting along in school is hard. What part do you do best?" Mom shows good listening skills in order to hear the whole story

Greg: "Best? Oh, lunch time, I guess."

Learning strategies for a lifetime.

Greg believes if only he could get through school, the demands to "remember all that stuff" would be over. Adults know that new learning tasks are always coming up both on the job and at home. Many of the specifics of school lessons will be forgotten, but the means for finding and learning them again will prepare Greg and his classmates for most challenges.

Students with good learning and test-taking habits (see page 61) will always have an easier and more enjoyable experience with each new opportunity in both their work and home life. And school is such a large part of a child's life that if it isn't going well, it clouds almost all other activities.

Greg pointed out several sources of trouble when he said he was bored because he didn't see the use of math, couldn't remember the geography, and "the kids don't like me." Let's start with Greg's boredom.

> School is such a large part of a child's life that if it isn't going well, it clouds almost all other activities.

Kids who say, "It's boring," are sending a confusing message. They could mean that interest is low, and they don't see the need, or they could mean they are bored because they can't keep up or, the opposite, they are too far ahead. Parents need to sort out these meanings before they react.

The poor student who finds school lessons of "no use" usually means he finds no importance *for him* in the tasks that are requested of him: "Why should I do that? It's just busy work." A parent could be misled at this point and start explaining why *she*, the parent, thinks the work is important.

Mom: "Math is important, Greg, because one day you'll have to manage your own money and figure out shopping and other things in life."

Greg: "Uh, yeah."

Mom: "Also, you need it for the higher math when you get to college."

Greg: "Higher math? There's higher math??? I think I won't go to college."

Mom: "Don't talk like that. Of course, you want to go to college."

The "one-day-you'll-need-this" approach is not on target with Greg's original objection. His point was that the work is not important *for him*. Greg's value of the "you'll-need-it-for-college" argument is revealed when he suggests giving up college just to avoid math problems tonight!

Mom needs an approach to the meaningfulness and importance of a good education that is within Greg's short-range radar. It won't help to provide more arguments about, "You can't get anywhere without a good education," or, "Jobs will be harder to get, promotions will be harder to come by, and you'll end up with a hard life."

At the moment, Greg doesn't want, and can't have, those things. The "getting anywhere" idea seems like a probability statement of consequences too far in the future and too abstract. Anyway, the people on TV seem to do all right, some of them without much education, too!

How much education would a person need to earn the amount of money that Greg would think is enough?

So why should Greg study decimals in the fifth and sixth grade? What good is it to know portions of geography or American history? Why are spelling lists important? The answers need to be in the present activities of Greg's life. Remember he's a person on a short-term priority.

As he learns new things in school each day, Greg should be encouraged to use his new skills that day. Sometimes that requires real creativity on the part of the parent. Could Greg use his knowledge of decimals to keep track of the family checking account? Receive a fee for doing so?

If we have to drive to visit a friend, could Greg find the route on the map? If we want to leave a note, could Greg write it? If we have to add up the grocery list, could Greg do it? Count out the money? Take it to the store? Will he make costly mistakes? Yes. Couldn't he just stay interested in this stuff until he needs it later on? Probably not.

One mother I worked with showed how such skills are useful by taking her son to the bank with her. She allowed him to go in alone and pay the bills. When he returned with the correct change and explained it all, she gave him a "tip." Of course the tip might not be necessary for many children who would be happy with the importance of the task and trust they were given.

The "tip" is a parental judgment call, but he will never ask why he has to study arithmetic—he knows why. He also bakes for his mother. And when recipes need to be halved or doubled she does not interfere in the calculations. From bitter (and sour) experience he knows the importance of these skills. And he feels better about his own worth. He's not *just* a kid; he's a kid with useful skills that his parents respect.

Certainly a 10- or 12-year-old can handle a checking account for the family or plan and carry out the family food shopping. When he/she sits down to do it, you may hear, "I can't do this because I don't know decimals." Then you can say, "Oh, you need to add decimals! Let me go over that with you. Then you can carry on." Your child may not enjoy the process of learning decimals, but at least now he knows their importance. The greatest advantage in teaching is having a student with a reason to learn. When the decimals job is done, your child will know that reason.

> Remember that your chiild is a person with short-term priorities.

For school subjects that do not easily apply to daily tasks, parents can influence their children's respect for the subject by asking questions.

Mom: "What was your work in science today?"

Greg: "We numbered the chambers of the heart and followed a drop of blood through the system."

Mom: "I always wanted to know more about that. How does it go through?"

Show interest in school projects and point out, from news-of-the-day, where knowledge applies. Parent-child conversations that bring in schoolwork show the usefulness of the work and improve the child's respect for himself.

Many skills not covered in school are also important to learn. Cooking, washing clothes, caring for your room, and later on, car care. All tasks present opportunities for children to learn and gain some feeling of self-esteem as they become competent. The chores may be domestic ones that adults shun or view as burdens. But from a child's view they are, at first, new, and when the novelty has worn off, they still have the potential of letting the child be productive and helpful now.

> Chores provide opportunities for children to learn and gain self-esteem as they become competent.

Parents may be called on to show great tolerance as they allow practice with these important school-related tasks or tasks of everyday drudgery that parents could do faster. Calm your impatience with the knowledge that just mastering the task is rewarding to the child and insures the further benefit of a little self-pride. Mistakes are easier to tolerate for these activities because the benefit is pride as well as competence. When the task is closer to drudgery than to adventure, more enthusiastic praise will be needed.

Ordinarily a person gains little respect and takes little pride in doing drudgery. So when the child asks, "Why should I do this?" he may be beginning an argument, but he's also signaling his need for appreciation for doing the job. For activities that are not very important, fun, or adult, he's counting on you for support. His question about drudgery is telling you to focus on encouraging and praising him for a job well done.

Homework strategies that work!

Greg's second complaint about school showed up in geography. This time it wasn't so much that he questioned the usefulness of the subject by saying it's "boring" but he found it boring because he was not doing well.

Homework that requires staring at materials and trying to remember can be boring and it can be hard to keep up a good attitude. The problem requires a different parental approach:

Greg: "I just can't keep the states straight. We're supposed to know them by Friday!"

Dad: "What are they going to ask you about them?"

Greg: "We have to point them out on a blank map with no words or anything and name their capitals."

Dad: "Do you have a map?"

Greg: "I have the one in this book and I've been studying it a lot, but I don't remember much of it."

Dad: "How do you do the 'studying' part?"

Greg: "I look at the states and try to remember which ones go where."

Dad: "Greg, I think you need to go through a few drills in a situation like the one you're going to have Friday. How about tracing that map so we can have one that's blank like the one on the test. Then we'll make a few copies."

Greg: "OK, then maybe I could practice by filling in the names and capitals on the copies."

Studying requires practice. Greg has been trying to practice in his mind ("I've been studying it a lot"), but sitting and staring at a book or homework sheet is not real practice—performance of a behavior—and Greg has not made much progress. To make homework time successful, Dad first asks Greg what he is *doing*. Most students who are falling behind don't have a specific target for their effort. When they study, they stare at notes or books. They don't *do* anything.

Most of us don't have the kind of memory that retains a great deal from just looking; it's the *doing* that will be remembered. What do you remember from your high school days? Spelling? Math and vocabulary you still use (*do* things with)? But I bet you remember little of social studies, geography, history, or math you never use.

Practice makes almost perfect.

Many parents realize the importance of practice and tell their children to "work hard" in school. The "work hard" idea is good advice but it leaves out the specifics.

Successful work shows up in grades if the student is shown how the "work hard" idea is turned into active practice—not just staring at pages, but reading aloud; not just "trying to remember," but talking to others about the work, drilling important concepts, rewriting notes and important material, and drawing new diagrams or tables that organize facts differently. That's how the idea of "work hard" becomes successful learning.

If you are skeptical of this strategy, try the following experiment: Pick out a favorite magazine in which there are two articles or stories you have not yet read. Read the first story to yourself in your usual way. Find someone to listen to your report of the story or article and tell them all the detail you can remember—who wrote it, who was in it, what was going on, conclusions reached and so on.

Now go back to the magazine and read the second article or story. This time, stand up and read out loud, with good emphasis and inflection—to the wall if necessary. Now find your listener again and report this story, giving all the details you can remember of who, what, and where. By the end of the second report, you will notice how much more you remember of the second story. As one student said to me, "Well, of course I remember that one. I remember saying it!"

> Sitting and staring at a book or homework sheet is not real practice or progress in learning.

Reading assignments often lead the student to this mistake of leaving out the *doing* in learning. Many of my students have said, "I can't believe I did poorly. I went through (stared at) all the material for the test!" If you only read it (not really practice) and never use it, it will be gone soon. If reading is the assignment, have your student take reading notes, preferably on cards. For each page of reading the student should take some note. "Never turn a page without writing something," should be the rule.

The reading-note requirement has several advantages:

1. It is a source of motivation because it is a concrete product from which the student can take a feeling of accomplishment.

2. It is a product that the parent can encourage, review, and use as a basis for other rewards, if that's in the plan.

3. Most importantly, notes provide bench-marks of progress that allow the student to pick up at the right place after an interruption.

It's surprising how much studying is done in small sessions of only a few minutes between interruptions by phone calls, snacks, and other chores. Without a note-taking habit, most of us start again at the same place we started before. With past notes, we have a record of where we are, and we can move on to new material.

A last advantage of active studying comes at review time. A condensation of the work is available as notes, maps, tables, and drill sheets. This will guarantee the right material will be memorized, and your student can avoid the time-consuming misery of thrashing madly through unorganized material.

Strategies for tests

These test strategies bring positive results in either essay or objective tests.

During objective tests:

Certainly every student intends to answer each question, but very often items go unanswered. There are two reasons for this: fear of guessing and failure to remember the question. The student should carefully read *and eliminate* options. Checking off poor choices allows the student to focus on the remaining options and improve chances that small differences will be discovered. Once an answer has been selected, the student should read the first part of the item one more time to be sure that the selection is actually an answer to this particular question. Very often wrong options are, in themselves, correct, but not the answer to the question.

For essay tests:

The important guideline here is to answer each question twice—once in outline form and then as an essay answer. The student should write a brief outline on another sheet before beginning essay answers. This first answer can be in the student's own words and shorthand.

For example, in response to the question, "What was important about the Gettysburg Address?" the student might jot down, "Lincoln, at graveyard; during Civil War; trying to unite the country; said country must try hard to finish the war; for equality and people to run government; give quote."

Now, looking at the first answer, the student is likely to make the second answer complete and in good form. Also, as the student is writing the final answer, new points are likely to come to mind to add to the final answer.

The teacher is more likely to give a high score when the major points are easy to find. The teacher will also find major points more easily if your student's writing is as neat as possible. If this is a problem, buy an erasable ink pen before the next test!

Practice tests for students who "have trouble with tests."

If your student is concerned about a test, he should construct his own version, trying to make it similar to the test expected. Students often report that more than half of their questions were the same as the ones on the teacher's test! With those questions practiced in advance, the students easily remembered their answers and were quickly half-way to a good test grade.

The computer revolution in schools

Computer programs have expanded the variety of individualized drills for students. Also, the variety of examples of problem-solving tasks that attract students to challenges has been an advantage to teachers with tight schedules and pressures to provide individual practice. Math and language programs often have useful drills because the content of the drills and the tests that come up later are almost exactly the same. To select programs in other areas, where content can vary, you'll need advice from the school about *what* spelling, history, government, or social studies the computer program should cover.

Psychologists of the sixties predicted a revolutionary step forward for students because programs could highlight success when students answered correctly. The revolution has not reached the optimistic predictions of the "teaching machine" years.

The early psychologists felt that success with questions and answers would be enough incentive to keep the student working. But for many children, the novelty of working the screen wears off, and adult encouragements and real life applications are needed to keep up interest. It's the same support from parents and teachers that homework and lessons have always required.

Leaving a student on a chair, even one in front of a computer, will not produce the success we all hope for. Plan to continue regular contributions to computer learning in the form of home projects and specific encouragements.

A second limitation of computer effectiveness is in the action that is required from the student.

It's amazing to us adults that learning 3 plus 5 equals 8 on a computer doesn't result in a correct answer on every test paper after that. The student can make improvements with a computer program but how the improvement shows up on tests depends on how similar the evaluative test is to the program, not only in content, but in the way the student is asked to provide answers.

Here's another place you can contribute: make up some tests. Arrange to collect information from your child's school about what the classroom test will be. Then, you can construct practice tests on the computer material using the format and style your student will encounter at school. Perhaps your student could make up these practice tests. Quizzes and drills with pencil and paper will give your child practice expressing the answers as required later when no keyboard is around.

Tips about social problems

When school starts, better than half of the 75 million students will show up at a new school. Many will be new to a grade school, others new to a middle school or high school; some will be switching from home schooling to regular school; many will be the new kid in town.

Their friends are scattered among strangers. The conversations are likely to be one and two-word phrases. Being alone can be embarrassing. Those who are back for another year are likely to stick with kids they know, which leads to the impression of cliques and makes breaking in even harder.

How can a parent help his or her child make friends in this situation?

Mom's help could start with the nature of good friends. Your almost-teenager may need a glimpse of how it looks from the other person's side. A short exercise writing down a friendship list might raise some interesting questions. This should be a one-on-one situation, not a family activity with siblings. Siblings will add the competitive element.

Your student should start her friendship list solo with only her thoughts and just a little help from you. Help her talk about or, if she's older, have her write down, "What makes a good friend?" Both sons and daughters will probably list, "Someone who likes me, someone who listens to me, and someone who is available." Now ask him or her to write, "And so to be a good friend, I should…"

Answers to this second part can stimulate useful talk. The kids may discover they really don't like the example set by TV's Mr. or Ms. Cool who is sarcastic and critical of others. Such people may make interesting characters on the tube, but the quick comebacks and criticisms don't make for close friendships or a warm family life.

While waiting and hoping to be admired themselves, kids often neglect the other person's yearning for a few kind words. Regardless of his pretensions, even that nasty kid secretly hopes for praise.

The following tips can help your children practice the social skills they will use all their lives.

Tip No. 1: Learn how to listen.

In the din of school noise and chatter, everyone wants to be heard but most kids feel nobody is listening and may notice that nobody is even looking at the ones who are talking. Make an effort to look at friends when they are talking. You don't want to stare, but if you look away too much, the other person thinks you don't care. Your eyes, your reaction, and your preoccupation with your handheld phone say a lot about how you feel. Friends need friends to listen.

Tip No. 2: Find something to like.

The art of the subtle compliment is to like something about the other person. Are they funny? Smile at them. Do they have a story to tell? Nod occasionally and show interest in what they have to say.

Tip No. 3: Take extra time.

It's easy to just "run over" what others have to say. Everybody's rushed and anxious to get in what they want to say. Slow your talking pace and pay attention.

Middle school and high school are big steps even if the kids seem to belittle the challenge. Just a month or so ago, they were the oldest kids in school. Next month they will be the youngest again. With many more teachers, classes and older kids to imitate, your child will probably be in culture shock. You will have a lot to talk over this fall.

Visit the new school this summer—if only to walk around the outside. This will help ease your child's first-time jitters, even if he has been there before.

Sometimes people argue that the performance of good students proves that problem students can also shape up. But we know habits change only for important reasons such as new encouragements for reasonable goals. Threats, reprimands, and coercions are temporary ways to shape up students. But if we could get the poor student consistently going right, he/she would have a good chance of encountering good results and then continuing. We need a way to get that first turn-around to work:

> **Friends need friends to listen.**

Ian: "I like war books."
Media Specialist: "I know you do, but what about those homework papers you need to do?"
Ian: "Oh, I'll never catch up, so why keep trying?"
Media Specialist: "Well, I'll give you a reason, Ian. For every finished homework paper you show me, I'll find one of those books you're interested in. Choose an easy paper first so that you will have some success right away."

This strategy helped Ian catch up in one of his classes, but shouldn't Ian get the practice of looking up his own books in the media center? I think in this case the need requires concrete rewards to get important behavior going again. The use of an easy homework paper as a starting point was also a good suggestion.

If your student is "having trouble with the teacher," counselors often use the next few suggestions to help students improve their classroom habits.

1. A student influences a teacher's attitude just as a teacher influences a student. When there is a choice, your student should sit in a seat as close to the front as possible and keep good eye contact with the teacher during presentations, just as you would practice good listening skills in a private conversation.

2. Your student should be alert for a question to ask. A continual banter of unnecessary questions will do no good, but good questions help learning *and* teaching. Einstein's mother used to ask him when he came home from school, "Did you ask any good questions today?" If your student tries to ask good questions in class, he has reasons to follow the teachers' presentations more closely and is more likely to learn.

3. Your student should occasionally talk to the teacher about the

subject after class. Some people may object to the contrived nature of this suggestion, but many children have the mistaken notion that the classroom is, or should be, a place where completely passive learning takes place. The student needs to know that an active, assertive role is necessary. The fact is that a classroom is a social situation where exchanges are a part of the learning. Warming your relationship with your teacher will improve your active learning and *that*, in turn, will improve grades!

A Harvard professor I know always distributes a slip of paper to each student before class. The top line on the slip reads, "The *main point* of the day was . . ." followed by a space for the student to complete the statement. The next line says, "My question for today is . . ." followed by more writing room.

> **Your student needs to know that an active, assertive role is necessary.**

The professor collects the slips each day from the students who have completed them. He reads them to see how the main point has been understood and what confusion is in need of more attention during the next class.

Students must think, summarize, and question. The professor has excellent feedback. Many professors now use this procedure. Even before your child goes to Harvard, the question-and-answer game can help schoolwork.

Try this practice:

Explain that you are going to play a question and answer game related to the media and school.

1. The parent picks a science news show, program, or written article heard or seen lately, and makes up a question about the information. For example, "This morning I read an article about the eclipse tonight. Why doesn't it happen all the time?"

2. Now, it's the child's turn to ask a question about school subject material. Have him choose classes in which learning needs to be improved. For example, if geography is a problem, he could ask: "Can you point to a place on the map where four states come together?" It is not necessary to answer each question, but if this happens, it's a plus to the main goal of the game, which is to focus on the usefulness of each subject or media item. Repeat the game occasionally with different school subjects.

3. A follow-up to the game is for the child to ask questions in classes at school. Compliment your child for questions and encourage discussion about the information. If your child didn't ask a question, have him/her write the ones that would have been best to ask.

EXERCISE
To observe what's happening, start a behavior chart

Fill in the seven steps of a "Behavior Chart." This exercise creates "behavior charts" so that the questions of what happens next and where to place the blames and credits will be clear in your mind when the troublesome situation comes up. You may need to return to this exercise to make new behavior charts as you focus on new situations. For this first session, examples are provided for each part. A blank behavior chart is presented on page 205.

Step 1: Describe the problem objectively.
Often this provides more help for the parent than other parts of the exercise. Just putting down what exactly is bothersome allows Mom and Dad to pick their attention targets and find room for positive support when it is deserved.

Example: Trevor always disrupts dinner, makes noises, cries, complains about the food, and wants down off his chair.

Step 2: What triggers the action?
Think back to the last few times the problem in Step 1 happened. What started it all? Who was involved? What time of day was it? Does this always occur in a certain part of the daily routine—bedtime, meals, or when siblings are absent?

Example: Happens when dinner is late and I give him something to "hold him over." Or, "Didn't happen when his sister was at Grandma's."

Step 3: What happens next?
You may have to think back to the last moments of the problem to remember exactly what ordinarily happens right after the troublesome behavior. Long-term consequences can play a role, but we need to understand the immediate effects first.

Example: We usually try to get him to eat, tell him to stop acting up, sometimes let him down since he just dawdles along and makes trouble anyway.

Step 4: Where would you place the blames and/or credits?
Sometimes this part will not apply to the subject at hand. But often

an objective statement about where each person thinks the fault lies will direct us to action without having to badger the transgressor with blame.

Example: He's just trying to get attention and he eats junk between meals. It may also be a power game.

Step 5: At what age would you expect an average child to do what you are hoping will be done in this situation?

Don't skip this part. Often when parents consider the age they would expect an ability to develop, they realize they are ahead of the child's schedule in their demands and expectations of him.

Example: He's four. He should be able to eat at the table without making extra trouble.

Step 6: How could we allow more practice?

Is it possible to provide more opportunities for the child to try out appropriate behavior with your loving support handy?

Step 7: When do things happen?

Keep a record similar to the one in the back of the book. A short record of what's going on and the effect of your reactions is often a good starting place for pinpointing a problem. Set out a sheet of paper similar to the one on page 204 and try to keep a record for a week so that you can review a good sample of the action.

> Multiple copies of the behavior chart could be made from the example on page 205

Chapter 3
"I love you" is not much without "I like you."

Who but a parent would ever take the trouble *to look* for opportunities to admire the little successes? Even a spouse, if you are lucky enough to get a good one, will not *seek out* your good points. If your good points show up, your spouse may express appreciation, but a parent is the only super friend with love enough to *look* for good points.

Parent who have to enforce the limits can't always be buddies, but in celebrating progress they can be the best kind of friend.

These kinds of friends bring out the best in me. I like the "me" they draw out. When we meet, their attention sweeps the common ground between us looking for sparkles to highlight. I return the compliment. Like a friendly searchlight, my job is to find the gems!

Parents and their children should be friends. Not in the sense of enjoying the same music or having friends in common or playing similar roles in the family, but in the sense of enjoying time together, and like a friendly searchlight, looking for sparkles and supporting the strengths in each other.

Some people have another focus. Their search overlooks the good we try to provide and zeros in on vulnerable spots. We pull back, risk very little because we know what they're looking for. We cover up.

Aim *your* searchlight carefully. What are you looking for?

Parents send a lot of messages. Every time the kids do anything, the parents react—negatively or with support or with indifference. Even indifference is a kind of message. So what a parent likes and doesn't like about what's going on is almost constantly expressed. Loving, on the other hand, is often limited to bedtime or other rare moments, *"Goodnight. I love you."*

So how does the liking get delivered? We all know very well what bad behavior is: fussing, doing dangerous things, fighting, making messes. But the words we use for good behavior are often less specific: be nice, act right, do well in school. Not having an exact idea of what good behavior should be, we often only find, and comment on, what we *don't* want: don't make trouble, don't yell at your sister, don't fight with your brother.

But what's a child *to do*? What should a parent look *for* in a child's choices of action? When, for example, does "not fighting" deserve support? Better to think of positive specifics—help with setting the table, saying something complimentary to his sister, giving her brother a toy he's been looking for. The exercise on page 97 will help you create your own list of likes

Of course we love our children. But how can children *know* if their parents *like* them? How much do we like them? They learn about that from the accumulated parental reactions to what they do, and they are always doing something! We update our message frequently in our reactions to our child's behaviors everyday:

Mom: "Leave Baby Mark alone, Nathan."

Nathan: "I was just going to pat him."

Mom: "I know what you were going to do. Now just stay away, you'll wake him."

Or, she might have said, "I like to pat him, too. But it will just wake him up and he's tired."

(Nathan drops his jelly sandwich)

Mom: "You are so messy! Look what you did!"

Or, she might have said, "Oh, look what happened. Better get a paper towel and pick it up."

If Mom chooses her first impulse, she emphasizes Nathan, the person. *You* will wake him, *you* are messy. If she chooses her second thought, she emphasizes a third thing that *she and Nathan* are dealing with together: *It* will wake him. Look *what* happened.

It won't make a lot of difference to Nathan on these two occasions. But over the long haul, Nathan ends up with a very different message and a very different relationship with Mom.

Emphasis on the defects can be a discouraging punishment. Jovial and approachable people seem to never punish. They have a rule that says, "When mistakes happen, emphasize *outside* events." To the extent that they must correct, contradict, reprimand, and punish, they risk losing this friendly air.

This can be the reason some growing daughters and sons become alienated from the family and would rather go outside with friends or stay in their own rooms. It's the likelihood of criticism, "put downs," and corrections that drives them away—just as it does Mom and Dad.

    Mom: "John, sometimes I wonder if you really like me, you criticize me so much!"
    Dad: "Honey, I *love* you!" You know that."
    Mom: "That's different and it's not what I hear during the day."
    Dad: "What? You want gush with mushy stuff all the time?"
    Mom: "No, I just want the benefit of the doubt. I want someone on the lookout for my good points and my successes. I've already got plenty of critics in my world!"
    Dad: "You have *plenty* of good points."
    Mom: "Then point them out now and then."

Praise, encouragement, and genuine friendliness are no doubt the most effective influences spouses have on each other —and parents have on their children. When these reactions are part of the habits, the directions about the right way to go are clear. Your child attracts your attention easily—for good or bad behavior. Selecting what *should* attract your attention, and what should not, sets the direction of a child's search for what's right.

Selecting behaviors to support with positive attention is the main business of being a parent. The exercise on page 97 can help keep the most attention on the best behavior. Your habits are contagious and your attention is the main part of the family atmosphere. If looking for mistakes becomes the routine, parents become unpleasant when doing the parenting job and don't like themselves as they do it. The family atmosphere follows that mood. The children will respond in kind, recycling the wrong attitude.

Children engage in a conspiracy—almost unconsciously—to show you that you are having no effect. They don't have the insight or assertiveness for conversations like the one above between Mom and Dad. But don't be misled. Your influence may not show up in the short run, but your reactions do make *the* difference. Don't give up. Watch a certain behavior for a few weeks to test your influence and notice how upset they get when they feel ignored! Attention, praise, and general encouragement are handy rewards. They should be used often.

Vague expectations about good behavior and specific descriptions of bad, lead to unbalanced parental messages that say "I don't like you (or your behavior)" more often than they say, "I like you." Bad behavior may attract most of the attention because the "good" behavior is not spelled out well enough to be easily noticed. Getting down to the specifics of good behavior leads to the following advantages:

1. **Parents become alert** to the smaller successes.
2. **Children get clear messages** about behavior.
3. **Parents provide good examples** of how to encourage others.
4. **Children develop and improve** with small easy steps instead of becoming discouraged by reprimands for small mistakes.

These four benefits contribute to a great parent-child relationship and should be a part of every day of childhood. The child longs for the joy and safety of it, and parents take satisfaction and pride in it. Your relationship is developing from a mixture of your understanding of what's going on, your messages, rules, listening, and example. Consistent strategies, planned with the help of other parents, are key ingredients in cultivating this relationship. Now, what are those guidelines that bring all of that together?

What guidelines could measure up to the task of preparing another person's future? Only ones that lead to learning and expression without fear of unjustified criticism; ones that will help us maintain a relationship that gives our children the self-confidence and self- esteem to be comfortable in childhood and competent in adulthood.

Basic heredity and personality will still show through childhood experiences, but a review of daily events can often be more useful because a parent can meet the needs, plan to withhold reactions, and deliberately provide a positive example. The suggestions in the previous chapters can help you discover your child's motivations and satisfy those wants with strategies that work toward growth and proper behavior through rewarded behavior.

The best outcome would be that we all get what we deserve, improve our behavior as a result, and are satisfied. In the real world, of course, some justice is done, but undeserved rewards do occur and satisfaction only happens to a degree.

The crucial question confronting parents is not whether rewards, punishments, encouragements, and discouragements should be used to influence a child's behavior; in day-to-day living that influence is inevitable. The question is whether parents will have time and love enough to plan some of these consequences so that the child will learn what needs to be learned and grow up properly.

Passing on social skills

My daughter once said to me, "You're doing that stuff you write in those books, aren't you? Can't you just be natural?"

I said, "Natural is good, but yes, I do think about what I say to you some- times. If thoughtfulness is being phony, I guess I'm guilty."

In spite of the complaint of being a little phony, kids need to learn that it takes effort to learn social skills. "Mom, how can I get the kids to like me?" can be a heart-breaking question. Can a parent provide any real help to a child with this worrisome problem? Yes, specific, practical suggestions can make a difference.

Jason: "So, Joey, how did your soccer game go?"
Joey: "What? Oh, it was OK."
Jason: "Must have been a mess with all that rain."
Joey: "Yeah, you should have seen the mud down at the goal; our goalie looked like a pig!"
Jason: "Our field still had some grass down there."
Joey: "Did you have to play that Kickers team?"
Jason: "Yes. Have you played them already?"

Jason has a good social habit of an occasional question. Most adults learn early that part of getting along is remembering to express some genuine, unselfish interest and *liking* for others.

Children and teens can be cynical and believe that being "likeable" is "inborn" and each of us must suffer with our inherited "personality." But most adults have seen a low responder like Joey "brighten up" or "turn around" with a compliment or question that shows interest in his life. How responsive and "attractive" Joey is might change. It depends on his companions *and his own effort.*

> **Part of getting along is remembering to express some genuine, unselfish interest and liking for others.**

Jason's attractive habit is often imitated and Joey, not usually outgoing, picks up the topic and finally has questions of his own. Jason partly creates his own pleasant social world. Both Jason and Joey probably like each other because of the habits they "draw out" of each other.

Being "likeable" is more than asking a few questions and just asking a few will not turn a person's social life around. But children and teens can easily get the priorities mixed up. They often put appearance first on the "Likeable Characteristics List" and put clever, cool, or funny conversation second.

The characteristic missing from the list usually shows up when the child or teen is asked *who he* likes. Usually, the answer is that he likes people who accept him, admire him, and want to spend time with *him*! Sometimes the view from the other person's shoes leads to the discovery that: "To be liked, I should make an effort and not be too critical." This would include habits of asking about the other person, showing some concern, being agreeable, complimenting, and giving time and companionship. These are the behaviors we look for when we try to teach a troublesome child about being "good."

Kids need to develop the inclination to be a friend instead of a critic. Without this inclination, the first social difficulty is usually frequent fighting, grabbing, or crying as a result of not understanding how to cooperate with fellow grade schoolers. A school bully at times has things his way (there's no problem when I get what I want!). If it doesn't go his way, he tries to punish the offending companion. Such a "me first" child is usually the first one that teachers, parents, and other children complain about.

Good plans, good changes, good consequences.

The most dangerous thing on earth is a human being with nothing to do. A child may not have the potential to cause as much havoc as an adult, but a child delayed from moving on to new challenges has a surprising ability to find trouble. That is one reason this book encourages you to start expecting (encouraging and rewarding) your child to make his/her bed, cook a meal, wash the car, look after his/her younger sibling, as soon as it is reasonable. Start early to build his/her self-esteem and for the sake of building abilities he/she can be proud of.

Parents are often hesitant in handing over the daily tasks of life for many reasons. They may feel a responsibility to do the chores themselves, and when they insist that the child take part, they feel guilty. Parents are often inclined to protect their children from drudgery as if it were an evil to be concealed as long as possible.

Completing the drudgeries of life is, in fact, one source of satisfaction that wards off depression. With children this benefit is often missed because the verbiage that goes with chores is usually negative. Both parent and child talk of "chores" as burdens to be carried. That's true, but the usefulness to psychological health should not be forgotten by the parent facing resistance from a growing-up child.

Boys, in particular, are subject to protection from chores and often suffer feelings of exasperation at having nothing "really worthwhile" to do. Remember a child probably wouldn't know what's "really worthwhile" if it bit him on his leg!

Parents need to teach these values like all others, by example, and by seeing to it that their son, as well as their daughter, gets opportunity and encouragement for his domestic efforts.

For a boy, there may be unrecognized sexism in being denied training for everyday chores. He may not know he is being short-changed. He may complain all the way through any chore requested of him. But his self-respect and his value of himself will be improved with every competence he acquires. And when he encounters a temptation to try some self-degrading or self-damaging behavior, he will be more likely to value himself and believe he has something to lose.

When an adult refuses, let's say, a drink at lunch, what is the most common excuse? "Sorry, I can't, I've got to work this afternoon, things to do." The self-evaluation is: "I have important things to accomplish (skills to use). I am too valuable!"

Allowing Practice.

We parents can plan situations to ensure our child has opportunities to successfully practice good social behavior. Mothers know that their children get cranky or tired at certain times. While it's true the child will eventually have to learn to control himself in all situations, let's start the training at a time of day when success and opportunity for support are likely. A child who is cranky before dinner and is just learning to control his temper with others, shouldn't have friends over in the late afternoon when probabilities for mistakes are high. An alternate plan might be to have dinner earlier, or lunch later, in order to give him a better chance for success. These alternatives are not strategies about reactions and consequences but merely rearrangements of the family schedule to improve success and reduce mistakes.

> **Start the training at a time of day when success and opportunity for support are likely.**

For example, parents and teachers know homework can be improved with scheduling and proper surroundings, and teachers and PTAs encourage parents to provide a quiet and private place conducive to doing homework. These kinds of arrangements are important for many situations beyond just homework. Accidents at meal time can easily be influenced by the way the situation is first set up. If a child is given a glass of milk too full, a cup of juice too hard to handle, three utensils when he only uses one, five foods to play with when he never eats three, and is then seated on two slippery telephone books, the family is set up for an unhappy dinner of trouble right from the start. The goal may be to get him to eat properly with these disadvantages, but the training will have to start with a better chance for success.

If all of this seems to be too much trouble, maybe it's time to rethink just how serious the dinner problem is. These reactions may seem too extreme because it's "just not *that* important" when the parents give the problem serious thought. Maybe changing eating habits, for example, is not worth giving up all dinner time pleasantness and everybody should eat what they want of what is served. Children, adults and creatures of the earth will pick a fairly good diet on their own if it is available and sugar is subtracted from the temptations.

Have your support at the ready

When can you expect a child to learn without extra incentives? And until then, how do you find the right consequence?

The answer may lie in another question: "What would be the result if he or she did the task right?" This should be a frequent parental question: Has the problem come up because of a bad behavior or the absence of a good one? What are we looking for? What will we do when he gets it right? A parent with answers to these questions will know how to react and what to do when even a slight improvement pops out.

This leads to simple situations where the child is "set up" to be successful. And "success" will be the first small step toward the goal. Without this soul-searching for a ready incentive when the child is *slightly* successful, the little success may not be recognized and only complete triumph by the child (not likely) will produce a positive reaction.

If a plan for positive reactions accumulates success over a few weeks, then the next encourage- ments for the next success become easier to give; respect and positive expectation for what the child will do develop, and we are off to a better relationship. Without these timely positive reactions, parents are likely to become more and more impatient. Their level of expectation (what they are willing to reward) goes up, while their experience tells them that there is no improvement.

The level of expectation should be determined by what the parents know a child *will* (not *could*) do. But the frustration of no progress often leads parents to greater demands instead of smaller ones. This makes failure and parental disappointment even more likely next time.

No one wants to plan and control all their reactions to their child, but some planning and control will provide progress. The planning needs to consider how the consequences will be controlled. For example, TV time could be a positive incentive for getting homework done. Taking away TV time could be used as a punishment, but the effectiveness of this punishment will depend on what programs are available at the moment.

You can avoid this complication with a tally sheet that keeps track of TV time earned or lost. Then your son or daughter could cash in time from the tally sheet when he or she wants it. While the tally sheet procedure solves the problem, it has to be updated and attended or it will lack immediate effects. Time subtracted for bad behavior might not matter to a child at the moment because no desirable programs are on right now and other time may be left on the sheet anyway. Nevertheless, a tally sheet has many advantages in controlling the use of timed privileges. It can be used to keep track of weekly allowance, outdoor play, or any other measurable privilege you want to control as an incentive for the child's good behavior.

When privileges are controlled, it's important to make the rules with minimums and maximums you know you can keep. Rules with extremes that "really fix" his problem or "make him stand up and take notice" will probably be inconsistent. Set your standards so that you can apply the consequences with an easy conscience. You might want to set a minimum and a maximum amount of TV time each day so that your child's bad or good moments can't make an extreme situation that results in breaking the rules.

Support gradual changes.

Of course parents know that starting at perfect is not possible, but many believe they should withhold strong encouragement until good progress is made. A gradual approach, with encouragement for any effort, is more effective. To *guarantee* support of the very first efforts a person makes on a new task, we need a short-term target. Later we can add higher expectations by expanding the request or the range of circumstances.

Here's an example of the gradual approach: When I first met Samantha she would not talk in school. Her mother had come to see me because this only-a-little-troublesome habit had become a real problem with the requirement that in order to be promoted from first grade, she had to demonstrate reading aloud in class. Fortunately for Samantha, her mom, and for me, reading aloud was not part of the problem. Reading aloud was already easy for Samantha to do under another circumstance, at home with her mother. Samantha needed to bring her success to the school situation.

To do this, Mom began meeting Samantha in her classroom after school. With the classroom empty, Samantha would sit in her seat and read to her mother for a few minutes before they went home.

The following week the teacher stayed in the classroom, but was obviously occupied with work at her desk in front of the room. She took no notice of Samantha or the reading. In the third week, the teacher took more notice of the mother-daughter reading session, and by the fourth week she did nothing but listen to Samantha read. For a few more sessions Mom sat farther away and the teacher sat nearer. The last session took place before the other children had left the room, and Samantha's promotion to second grade was assured.

The procedure just described did not require new behaviors or complicated strategies. If Samantha had yet to learn to read, we would have had a much bigger problem, requiring many more steps along the way. We might start with identifying pictures or letters, providing some phonics training, adding simple words to the lessons, and so on.

Whenever you use a shaping process like this, you must begin with a level of performance that occurs frequently so that the child can learn the rules and experience success right away. Even after some progress, backtracking may be necessary to keep the positive reactions high during the slumps in performance.

In nearly every case, the ideal behavior is not gained in one easy step. At first you will have to dig back to some low level of success or different circumstance. After that not-very-exciting level has been strengthened, the next level can be added with plenty of encouragement.

Here's another example. Amy came home with failure after failure on her spelling lists. Her mom's temptation was to drill her over the errors she had made and, although getting rid of the errors was the ultimate goal, this didn't do much to pump up Amy. The approach of "I'll show Amy all of her mistakes" ensures that rewards will be hard to come by and the results will be frustrating and embarrassing with frequent mistakes. It will emphasize how much Mom knows and how little Amy knows.

So I asked Amy's mom to start spelling sessions by asking Amy to spell words she had right on lists of the past weeks. Mom ran through those lists quickly, but she took time to note with pride and encouragement all Amy's successes. Then Mom mixed in a few of the ones that Amy had missed. Bolstered by some recent successes, Amy could tolerate her own errors and her mom's corrections. Mom would often come right back to one or two easier words. Mom manipulated Amy's success rate and kept it high by putting in as many "easy" words as necessary. A few 15-minute drills and Amy was finished with the week's spelling and was feeling good about herself and about Mom.

Fading a brief performance to a long one.

Jeffrey is another example of starting where encouragement is probable. Jeff's mother complained to me that he couldn't sit still in school, keep his attention on his work, or stay out of trouble with other students. The prospect of long-term consequences (grades, threats of failing, being held back) had no effect on him.

By using the technique of focusing and defining the desired good behavior, we could start with some aspect of Jeff's problem, building up the time he sat in his seat with incentive for doing so, then working on his attention span, and then his tendency to fight with other students. All this would be a long process.

But these behaviors are interrelated with the thread of Jeff's boredom so we may have to deal with them all at once—sit, work, stay out of trouble. The strategy with Jeff's teacher and parents was to concentrate on all three complaints at the same time, *but only* for a short period.

> **Either reward good behavior or not, but no arguments, no repeated explanations, and no threats.**

Each morning Jeff's teacher "checked in" with him as he arrived in class so that he had a little attention "in the bank" to start with. Then if Jeff stayed in his seat, paid attention, and didn't get into any trouble with others for the first 15 minutes of class, he would get a copy of a note Jeff's parents had printed for his teacher to use. It said, "Dear Mr. & Mrs. Jones, Jeffrey started school just fine today." More about the notes later.

The strategy for Jeff required him to take control of himself all at once—quite a challenge and one that seems to violate our notion of very small steps to guarantee reward at the very beginning. But in Jeff's case we are quite demanding right from the start, but only for a *very short time*, which makes it possible to deliver on the reward very quickly. Nothing

Jeff does during the rest of the day can take away the precious note which is about how he *started off* his day.

Because it was difficult for Jeffrey's parents to deliver encouragement and support in the classroom where the success might happen, we used a part of the idea of a "token economy." We are all familiar with this idea in our own lives. You work for tokens, something that is only a symbol of the value it can be exchanged for. In the real world, money is a symbol we work for.

Jeff knows about money, too, but he has an extra token—the note from the teacher. Jeff was told, "If you stay in your seat, pay attention, and stay out of trouble for the first 15 minutes of class, Mrs. Norton will give you a note, and you can use that note for extra playtime, TV time, or extra dessert at home after school."

Jeff found more than one use for his notes and wanted more. In the following weeks, the teacher supplied a second note for the second 15 minutes. In week three, the interval was changed to 20 minutes and two more intervals were added for the first 40 minutes after lunch. Now Jeff could get a maximum of four notes—tickets of admission to extra activities at home—each day.

> **Emphasize the admiration, encouragement, and usefulness of your child's learning because contrived rewards can't go on forever.**

We didn't want to complicate the teacher's procedures so Jeff's parents made up the notes and delivered them to her. And we didn't want to give extra attention to Jeff for being bad. Therefore, the teacher refrained from discussing Jeff's mistakes in class. He either got the note or he didn't—no arguments, no repeated explanations, and no threats.

Of course, a system like this can't be kept going for a long time. Jeff will get tired of it, his parents may get tired of thinking up new privileges, and the teacher certainly has enough to do without continuing this rule for a long time. The usual results of good school behavior are going to have to take over and keep Jeff on the right track once we get him started. The natural results or admiration, encouragement, and usefulness of his learning need to be emphasized, because we know the contrived reward can't go on forever.

There are three important points of caution here. First, the teacher must be consistent and keep in mind a clear definition of what 15 minutes of good behavior is. Second, Mom and Dad have to play the game strictly with Jeff. And third, Jeff must understand from the beginning that the rules will change along the way.

Jeff's case required a lot of effort from several people. They carried through and Jeff has become a much better student as a result. The planning, conferences, notes, and activities at home acknowledge that the notes were worth something. All these things take time and effort. So as you think about your own children, you have to ask yourself an important question: "Is this a problem that deserves my effort?" Many times, as you think this question through, you may want to change the complaint or scratch the problem off your list altogether.

Once some new level has been reached, the problem is how fast to move along. Feedback and support can grow stale rapidly if you don't move on to a new and challenging target. Also, dwelling too long at one stage can make it difficult to move on later.

Caution about slow fading.

Consider the parent who praises baby talk long after it has been mastered. It was a necessary first level, and of course support for these early efforts is just good parenting. But the longer the child continues baby talk, the more likely he is to discover that some people will always find it cute and attractive. Also his parents become very practiced at understanding it and inadvertently reward the almost unintelligible requests.

These complications have their counterparts in eating, dressing, and "baby" social skills—selfishness, possessiveness, and lack of consideration for others.

Instead of moving too slowly, take a more flexible view of child-rearing that says, "When in doubt, move up to a new level of expectation for awhile. You can always move back again, if necessary."

> **Provide situations where your child needs to "know these things" now.**

One of the most common reasons for hesitating to move up is that the next step involves real consequences for the parent. After a child has learned to count money and make change, he is ready to go shopping, probably with your money! This is a very dangerous time for hesitation on your part because this is when the child learns whether or not the skills are really useful and part of growing up, or just boring preparation for growing up later. We can't expect a child to be eager about your instruction, or the school's instruction, if he's only told "Someday you'll need to know these things." Provide situations where he "needs to know these things" now.

In these later steps, a parent's role changes. The parent has prepared the child to some extent for the outside world and now the world provides more and more of the consequences. But you still have an important duty. Now your job begins to resemble a coach's job. You're not in the game any more providing consequences; you are more often on the sidelines giving advice, pointing out what happened and where the consequences are coming from.

The crucial point to remember is that this change of duty doesn't happen at a particular age, but for particular skills. You may finish giving planned lessons for toilet training by four; hopefully you'll be finished with eating behavior by eight! Really?! And you may still be working on money management at 17 and social skills at 25!

A "catch 'em being good" rule puts parents on the lookout for their children's successes and the good behaviors that will allow them to give more support. These successes are usually just small parts of the larger habits of their children. For example, considering how to encourage a child who is "shy" is a complex problem because such an over-used and abstract concept of a person does not specify the little events from the average day that make up the impression of being shy. It is too large and covers too many emotions and habits.

We need to know what behaviors to look for in order to pinpoint what is worrisome and when to react. Without the pinpointing, the temptation is to try to *talk* the child out of being "shy." "Oh, come on. There's nothing to be afraid of here!" "Just say hello." "Go over with the others."

If the shyness problem is restated in specific terms: "He doesn't talk very much," or "She hides when company comes," or "He likes to play alone," then the appropriate reaction to each of these habits can be worked out. That way, parents will know when they want to encourage change (we'll encourage her a lot when she has something to say) and when to avoid the risk of embarrassing, unwanted attention (playing alone is OK).

Also, focusing on a few good behaviors replaces the habit of blaming the whole child, "putting her down," and sending the message that she should be ashamed of her own personality.

What reactions can be expected if the child does "come out of her shell?" Shyness produces some attention and little reprimands and excuses. What does non-shyness produce?

A careful parent might plan some mild encouragement and even practice what could be said in a planning session, "That was a nice 'Hello.'"

With a plan to provide attention for those non-shy moments, things might improve for the patient parent. A shy child's request to get away from a visitor might be answered with, "OK," avoiding additional talk by the parent to get her to stay or by the child to get away.

Learning to practice and practicing to learn

Anyone who has ever tried to play a musical instrument, improve in a sport, or raise children knows that just talking about it is not enough. Readings, lectures, and memorizing rules can help, but real practice is crucial. Even golf has helpful hints and rules to learn, but golfers know the only way to improve is through practice.

All golfers know players who still search for the magic gadget or secret technique for success while they avoid practice time. The notion applies equally well to social behavior, controlling anger, getting along with siblings, homework, tooth-brushing, and money management!

So helping a child listen and pay attention to advice is not enough. He will have to try out your instruction, test your rules, and then, if the consequences and encouragements are there, he will learn. The progress itself—the result—will come from practice.

This is the main role of a family—to provide a place where successful practice will be supported and mistakes will receive mild reactions—not a likely experience in the outside world. The family should provide an opportunity for safe practice without cruel punishment for mistakes and with a person who cares enough to support small successes. Supportive family members will be hard to come by when a child-teen grows up.

For learning and changing habits, there is no substitute for active practice. On your vacation, stare at pages in a novel while lying on the beach if you enjoy it, but if it's something to be learned for work, take along a notebook and pen to practice the main points.

Practice applies just as well to bed-making, dish-washing, and manners in society. If you, as parent, do these jobs for your children, there is no practice. It is easy to be overprotective and slow down learning: "I'll cut the meat," "I'll pour the milk," "I'll read, you listen," and "I'll call and see if your friend can come over—you wait."

Some parents will protest that if they let their child do these things, mistakes will happen. She might cut herself while cutting the meat, spill the milk, waste time reading instructions, or say the wrong thing on the phone. All true. And each parent will have to make the judgment—is she/he ready? Not, "Is she ready to be perfect?" but, "Is she ready to gain *something* from practice and mistakes?" We shouldn't wait until she's ready to do it perfectly. Without practice, that time may never come.

Another advantage to early practice is that your child can gain much to be proud of *now*. We can't give a steak knife to a two-year-old or a gallon of milk and a small glass to a four-year-old, but we can set up practice situations that guarantee opportunities for encouragement and praise.

A wise parent creates practice, not just for learning, but to improve the child's self-respect. A butter knife for the bread, a small pitcher for milk, a chance to "read" (tell about) the picture in a story, and call a friend just for fun—all of these are steps that promote learning and increase self-esteem.

Use small steps and big rewards.

When you were growing up, practice seemed to be enough to perfect your handwriting. And yet in learning to play a musical instrument, you may have found that even practice was not enough. What are the differences between your brief piano experience and your "learned forever" handwriting?

> **It's not the pot at the end of the rainbow that keeps the practice going, it's the next pat on the back or penny in the bank. Parents need to be frequent and generous back-patters.**

In learning to improve your handwriting, you were rewarded not only for the hours of practice but also for the first little successes. You wrote your own name, a friend's name, then a secret message, a note to a friend, then a letter to grandpa. The improvements were useful, shared with others, and practice continued.

But too often the first improvements in playing the scale on the piano produce little or no admiration, seem of little use, and are a long way from the performance dreamed of.

Sometimes piano lessons are successful because learning a favorite piece or popular song was part of the early training. If that consideration was a part of your lessons, practice probably continued. If not, you may have quit, but I bet you remember to this day the pieces you liked, the ones that attracted some attention and that others enjoyed.

If rewards come early for the first little successes, then a child will want to practice more on other small steps. If only big successes attract encouragement and little improvements are ignored, a child can become discouraged along the way, "I'll never be *really* good."

It is not the pot at the end of the rainbow that keeps the practice going; it's the next pat on the back or penny in the bank—and for some tasks, parents need to be frequent and generous back-patters.

The most common error when beginning to teach something new is to demand too much for too little. The first steps need big rewards—not necessarily tangible goodies but plenty of encouragement. "This sounds like bribery," you might say. "Shouldn't a child do most of these things without contrived rewards—can't they do it just for the love of learning?" "Some children are good and do what is expected without 'rewards,' don't they?"

To answer these questions we need to realize that those good little children *were* rewarded—socially and with parental respect and praise—a great deal. Some children start early and do well, with plenty of encouragement. They perform so well that they receive a great deal of praise and a snowballing effect begins that is an advantage for years to come. If a child starts off with good encouragement and is well rewarded, he keeps going. If he keeps going, he is further rewarded.

Snowballing can work the other way also. Some children don't receive much attention for the first steps to good performance and learning. They don't expect rewards because few were given in the past. They might do just the minimum out of fear, but that's all and even that will disappear when the threat is gone.

So without someone providing positive feedback, the child misses out on encouragement. As the child falls further and further behind her parents' expectations, any performance that should have been encouraged earlier will be ignored because "She should have done that long ago." Now even meager attempts at catching up are discouraged. If her success is viewed as "too late," the "pay" may be nothing. Without some "pay" she will become even more discouraged and fall back even further.

Natalie: "These math problems are really hard."
Mom: "You're really getting into some hard stuff now." (See "Reflective Statements" of Chapter 1.)
Natalie: "Yeah, they take too long."
Mom: "You got the first one, you should show your brother."
Natalie: "Hey, Larry, look at this!"

Larry: "We did those last year."
Mom: "And they were hard, but Natalie got the first one."
Natalie: "I'll try one more."

Mom's intention here is to show respect for what Natalie has done so far and a little encouragement to show it off. Larry doesn't help much, but Mom remains on the positive side and Natalie puts in a little more effort.

Does this mean that all successful parents are secret bribers? No. First, "bribery" is unfair because it implies a situation in which a person is trying to corrupt another person to do something wrong and usually illegal. Second, a child is not expecting a "bribe;" just some positive recognition of her success.

Yet no one works for nothing. Some volunteers work for no money, but they receive satisfaction from the reactions of others. The reward may be as subtle as another person saying they are doing well or as obvious as salaries for Congress and fees for doctors and lawyers.

In the adult world of raises, benefits, and strikes, the importance of the consequences for our efforts is always number one. On one occasion a father rejected my suggestion for encouraging his son's homework saying: "He should be grown up enough to want to do the right thing without some payoff!" When it came out that Dad was on strike for more money *and* was getting support from a strike fund, his defense was that *he was an adult!*

Dad, with his experience and knowledge, felt he deserved a tangible reward (as well as admiration and respect). His son, without experience, success, or respect, was to take his responsibility for the love of it.

So in addition to practice, we need recognition, respect, and encourage- ment. With all the right ingredients, the success will come *and*, along with it, a bonus, self-respect.

Short-term benefits and long-term goals.

While sorting out what happens next, both immediate and delayed reactions need to be considered.

Mom: "Why does she go running out of the house without a jacket? She knows she gets a cold *every time!*" (Yes, but that's *later!*)

Dad: "My friend, George, is just like that at work. He snacks all the time, he's overweight, and he can barely climb a few stairs without panting. Someday he'll be a-death-due-to-donuts! Can't he see what he's doing to himself in the long run?" (That's later, also, and George gives in to the "right now.")

Teacher: "I run two miles every morning. Sometimes it's hard to get started on it, but I feel better afterwards." (Somehow this teacher resists the effects of inconvenience right now for a better feeling later. How does she do that?)

Brian: "It's a good TV night, but each time I attend my scout meeting, I get points toward a merit patch!" (Here's a hint about how long-term benefits work: there's a *short-term* benefit!)

Behaviors tend to follow the short-term benefits at the expense of long-term goals, but with a few positive experiences, long-term consequences can overpower temporary temptations especially if someone supports the effort. How can a parent help this process of considering the long-term benefits of good behaviors and the long-term problems of bad ones?

A common parental strategy is to try to talk a child into considering the long-term. Talk by itself is often not enough as most of us dieters know. We need some symbol of the long-range goal *right now*, a reminder that we are making progress—a daily chart with marks for successes, a record book, or diary. Children may need something more concrete such as stickers, buttons, scout badges or treats. If those little encouragements are given generously, they can affect the present behavior. Isn't that what compliments from the boss, new titles or privileges at work, promotions, and badges in the military are all about?

Many positive reactions in the here and now are not contrived tokens, badges, or promotions. They are simply people on the lookout for opportunities to compliment and praise the small steps of good habits. It's not an easy task to be so observing and responsive, but those who do it have a good effect. We all know how our morale is elevated by bosses who are positive and supporting and deflated by ones who only react to mistakes. When work and chores are only for long-term benefits, a "boss" needs to put in short-term encouragements that will keep up the good effort!

It's hard to like non-behaviors.

Be careful when planning consequences for *non*-behaviors. Rules that say, "If you *don't* do such and such (watch too much TV, act too shy, walk on the flowers, hit your sister) I'll reward you" are difficult. The time of the promised reaction may be too arbitrary. When does *not* watching too much TV happen? What exactly is "too shy?" Better to build your rule around the *alternative* to TV—something that happens at a particular time and gives you an opportunity to support your son or daughter at a particular moment, "You're working on your picture; it's really looking good!"

Non-behavior rules fail the specific time test and also fail to tell the child exactly what *to do*. The solution to the non-behavior complaint can be reached by searching for what the child *should* be doing. "Karen watches too much TV" needs to explore what Karen *should* do. Karen's parents would be at a loss to keep her busy every moment, but it's the *extent* of TV-watching that's the problem. Karen's parents could encourage a few alternatives to the tube.

Does this mean that Karen's parents should load up on toys, candy, and money to lure Karen away from TV? Probably not. Most parents have found these rewards to have temporary effects—except in the case of money which will become a bigger part of Karen's life soon enough without any help from us.

> **Emphasize the specifics of good behavior.**

For problems such as Karen's, we need to look around for something useful that we might encourage her to do that would have the additional advantage of making Karen feel a little more important. She might even be proud of doing some of the drudgery of life. How about dusting, setting the table, cooking, sweeping, cleaning, or painting. Painting? "But she won't do it right!" you might say. "She'll mess it up. Cooking? That must be a joke."

Of course it's true that you could do any of these tasks better than your child. To get it done right, do it yourself. But the purpose here is not to get it done right; it's the self-esteem, the learning, and the alternative to TV. How *well* the job is done is not the priority. Now don't forget to plan the consequences: your time and positive attention, and maybe a concrete reward.

While pursuing perfection, what happens to "liking?"

A mother in my office complained that her son, 11-year-old Jason, was always making mistakes—spills, falls, blunders, breaking things, fighting with his brother. He could never quite measure up to her expectations.

As a new routine for the week before our next meeting, I asked her to look for a success or two and compliment him on it. She said the moment would be hard to find.

"Think of it as part of your parental job: to find the good moments and highlight them," I said.

The next week I asked how the assignment went. "Oh, I found something and I told him I appreciated how he helped his brother, and you know what he said? He said, 'What's the matter with you?'"

Even though the first attempt didn't get a very appreciative reaction, we agreed to try another week. At the end of the second week Mom reported that she had complimented Jason on three different occasions for little helps around the house. He asked, "Mom, do you *like* me?"

"Well, of course I like you! I'm your mother!"

Jason said, "Wow." Eleven years old and he is surprised to find out his mother likes him.

Stories of family situations in which just the right remark changes a child's view are rare and often unrealistic. So the liking message has to be sent often. It will take many more weeks for the liking message to stick with Jason.

Bold messages that suddenly "get through to" a child are seldom accom- plished. What Jason comes to expect as a result of consistent experiences will shape his long-lasting patterns. So while looking for just the right action from your child for just the right parental reaction, show some liking of the best approximations that are part of everyday life.

> **To enjoy successful parenting, the search for solutions should always return to the question, "What happens next?"**

How will others treat your children? Most people will not treat your children any better than you do. You set the tone and the expectations. Others are likely to pick up that message, develop the same expectations, and give your child the same respect you do.

These other adults will also react to the collection of skills, presumptions, and attitudes your children have acquired *from* you. In your childhood, your expectations included your parents' attitudes, which developed your self-concept. Now you are passing that collection on to your children—modified by the valuable experience you want to add.

As you pass along your self-concept and your assumptions about your children, the kids will develop an expectation about how *others* will perceive them. This becomes a self-fulfilling expectation because they take with them a whole pattern of attitudes, assumptions, and habits that will tend to recreate, in their new social lives, the same social experiences they left behind.

Most people won't treat your children any *worse* than you do, either! People model each other and their reactions tend to create their surroundings. Each of us causes some people to fade away and others to draw closer. We feather our own social nest.

Children will pick up your model of how you treat each person. They will pick up your attitude, disposition, and the nature of your appetite for life. Then they are off to recreate their own social environment by reacting to those around them, presenting a certain model, and selecting, without much attention, people who confirm their expectations.

The hard work of parenting is to "handle" the children and influence their habits, but the responsibility is all the more awesome because parents also teach children what to expect of themselves as well as what to expect from others. So your children learn from your social style and the life philosophy it represents. They learn by imitation and by the way you handle problems in the family *and* they also learn an attitude toward *themselves*.

> **Most people will not treat your children any better than you do.**

For many years, child psychologists have searched for solutions to the problems of parenthood. Their searches have usually focused on the reasons children do the things they do—in their reactions to parents, to siblings and friends, and to school. If we knew the reasons, we could find solutions to the problems. The solutions would make life easier and we could enjoy parenting more.

But solutions have been difficult to come by because they seem buried in a maze of complicated questions concerning the genes children inherit, the importance of early experiences they have had, and the recent treatment they have encountered from parents and others. Even so, theories about child behavior may describe a possible explanation that may help you understand the situation. That will be helpful in choosing a reaction in a calm and loving way. The purpose of this book, however, is to look to the everyday applications and help parents find *practical* strategies for action at the moments when problems come up.

Parents cannot afford the common craziness of doing the same thing over and over and expecting to produce a magical new result! Instead, we could try a *new* reaction to a child's anger, for example, based on an analysis of the events that make it happen and the reactions that a child gets for "being angry." That is, what happens next? To enjoy successful parenting, the search for solutions should always return to the question, "What happens next?"

Searching the possible consequences for explanations allows us to discover how to use *our* reactions to a child's emotions. The more recognizable the emotion is, the more consistent the reactions to it can be and therefore the more consistent the child's experience and learning.

For example, parents can easily agree on when their child is attempting a non-emotional activity, say, walking, and so they know when to help. A description here is easy (whenever she stands up and moves her feet around). Parents usually agree on when to encourage her, and she learns the task quickly.

Parents often disagree, however, about whether a child is really angry, just wants attention, or is tired. Often, even one parent cannot decide how to interpret these emotions. How do you react to a moody child who seems "angry" if he might be "tired?" If a father wants the homework done he might decide that an angry child is really just a procrastinating child. A mother trying to get a child off to bed might decide that "angry" is really "tired."

Dad: "Amber sure gives us a lot of trouble at dinner."
Mom: "It's just that she's tired."
Dad: "She's set on ruining it for everyone, I think."
Mom: "It's a bad age."
Dad: "Well, bad age or not, I'm tired of it."
Mom: "What do you want to do, have her eat by herself?"
Dad: "No, but we should do something. I'm willing to have dinner a little earlier, if that will help, but I think if she messes up her food, we should take it away and give her just the one thing she's eating. If she's not eating anything, we should take it all away and tell her to ask if she wants anything; what do you think?"
Mom: "OK, but I think our rule should include her yelling and trying to get down as well as messing up her food. And after we take the food away we should wait, say two minutes, before we give her the one food she has been eating, if there is one."
Dad: "OK, let's try it, at least we'll both be using the same rule."

"I always felt I was not quite good enough"

Many parents have told me that while they were growing up, their parents always pointed out the room for improvement. "I always felt I was not quite good enough," was one father's comment to me while telling me he wrote a letter to his mother every week throughout the years that his own children were growing up. But each letter was criticized for leaving out some detail. "I wish she had said just once that she appreciated all the news; she never wrote me, she always called and pointed out that some story had been left out of my letters."

It is a shame that many never experience such deserved appreciation. But the greater tragedy is that while a parent holds back compliments, the kids become discouraged with the task and resentment sets in. It takes courage to overcome the disadvantage of parents who have been too stingy with their compliments.

A parent's short-term job is child-rearing, but the long-term goal is adult-rearing. To reach that goal, children need examples of how adults handle their responsibilities and accomplish their tasks. But the kids are not adults yet, and left to their own inclinations, they may miss their chances to learn. They need time just following along while the adults show them the ways of the world.

> **It takes courage to overcome the disadvantage of parents too stingy with their compliments.**

Given too many choices, children may lean toward the wrong answers to questions about what to do. Questions such as, "What should we do today?" "Do you want to go shopping for food?" and "Would you rather watch TV or help me change the baby's diaper?" can be too big a challenge. It might be better to suggest the answer, "Come with me and help me at the grocery store."

Leaving a child out of the daily demands risks the loss of the adult example and teaching. The skills missed leave a void where a feeling of pride and usefulness could be developing. Protected from this education, they will feel less useful and less valuable.

Of course all members of the family need some times when they have it their way. But productive learning is more likely when adults do the leading. In *The Gesell Institute's Child Behavior*, you are advised to "try to provide, so far as you can, the kind of situation in which each kind of child can feel comfortable and do well. But don't try to change him or make him over." The advice is good except you are not yet told what the "kind of situation" is. The best situations will be ones where children learn by adult example and adult instruction.

The advice from the Gesell book also includes a caution to avoid trying to make your child over. This is confusing since we are working for some change. Just how far can we go and not be accused of "making him over?"

The way in which a child grows into the independence and competency of adulthood varies from family to family, and we all know that the extent of success varies also. We could probably agree that, ideally, child-rearing should be a process of gradually expanding responsibility and independence. Unfortunately, we have all seen many families where the children go through a long period of severe limits followed by an abrupt and risky freedom at about the age of 17 when the American teenager is sprung from the nest to go to college or work.

Mom: "I need some help with dinner every night. Neal. Could you set the table for everyone each night?"
Neal (age 5): "Do I hafta? Make Dawn do it"
Mom: "No, since she turned 9, Dawn makes the whole dinner on Tuesdays and lunch on Saturdays. You can set the table."
Neal: "I'd rather make a meal like Dawn."
Mom: "OK. Let's work on a few meals together, maybe we could start tomorrow night. But for now, do the table. That will be a great help!"

I am sure Neal isn't completely happy with this new chore, but with the proper appreciation, he will have an additional feeling of worth and ability. Dawn is learning she can take care of herself and Neal needs to learn the same.

Once away from home, our offspring-now-sprung will have to learn to make meals and car payments, avoid the pitfalls of credit cards and checking accounts, and leave time to enjoy life, but not too much time. We had better get started now teaching some of the complications of life.

Most children-turned-teenagers grow up late, painfully, and abruptly, but they grow up. Unfortunately, the newspapers tell us about many young adults who do not cope well with their sudden plunge into independence. As a result, many "children" come back home to live a few more years in the nest—not always a welcome idea to parents.

Mom: "Neal [age 12 now], maybe you could balance the checkbook each month this summer."
Neal: "What? I don't know anything about that!"
Mom: "Now's the time to learn. Maybe you should earn a "service charge" for the job."
Neal: "I'll try. But don't get mad if I get it wrong."
Coping well with the demands of bank accounts, budget

management, and the need to plan a future beyond the end of the month requires a great deal of practice at the younger ages.

While parents usually talk to their offspring about the demands of the outside world, it is easy to forget to allow practice with as much of that reality as possible. As soon as reasonable, children need experience with the freedom to make decisions on their own and reap the consequences of those decisions.

When they are successful, the protection of the family nest can make sure that the success is recognized and encouraged. The failures can be learning experiences with the consequences softened by the parents. A long period of safe trial and error is possible for children whose parents allow for it.

"Paying no attention" requires a plan

In the trial-and-error stage of learning, no reaction to mistakes may be a good idea, but this requires a plan to support the good behaviors; otherwise, new undesirable behaviors can creep in. For example, if Jimmy (age 3) has tantrums and Mom lets Jimmy cry it out, he may only change his tantruming style slightly.

Tantrums provided Jimmy with a way to get his portion of consideration. When that no longer works and there is more pressure on Jimmy to find another way to get the attention he wants, we're back to the circumstance that produced the problem in the first place. Mom and Dad need to plan some behaviors to encourage and reward.

For example, Kim was a fourth-grader who took up to four hours each night to complete the small amount of homework she was assigned. It was usually about a half-hour's work, but Kim continually prolonged her work. She had to get another pencil, go to the bathroom again (trip number three), get another paper, start over, etc. To understand the problem, the question "Why?" has to again be reworded to, "What happens next?"

What reaction does Kim get for losing her place and then finding her place or deciding to start over because of a small smudge on the paper? It's tempting to say she's particular or she is a perfectionist, and that might be true. But before we decide that the problem is inside Kim, let's look at the results of her procrastination, not at school, but right there where it happens.

The immediate result for Kim turned out to be the prolonged attention from an exasperated mother intent on Kim finishing her work.

When I asked, "What would happen if Kim suddenly finished quickly?" Mom said, "That happened! And I had dinner ready on time that night!"

If Kim did her work efficiently, Mom was gone in a flash to the kitchen. But if homework took a long time, Mom stayed around.

The solution to Kim's problem may seem easy at first. Just do nothing, and remove attention for all this procrastination. But Kim is working (procrastinating) for Mom's attention and it would be wrong to ignore that need and do nothing. Kim needs an acceptable way to be heard, attended, and considered in the family.

So the discovery that Kim is procrastinating for Mom's attention required more than a plan for restricting Mom's attention for this. Mom's new strategy was to give Kim help from 4:00 to 4:30 each afternoon for homework, then Mom did other things. After dinner, time was reserved for Kim to talk with Mom or Dad and do other activities besides homework.

At first, there were problems because Kim was still on homework after dinner, but after a week the family evenings had improved. Homework time dropped from four inefficient hours to 45 minutes of productive work. In addition, Mom remained alert to other possible activities for Kim that deserved more attention. Kim started helping with dinner and Mom showed her appreciation.

Merely removing attention from Kim was not the aim of the strategy. The "do nothing" strategy was actually a plan to look for *more* possibilities for paying attention to Kim. Completion of homework was still on the list but help with dinner and other evening activities made a more balanced and healthier list.

The child's view of the adequacy of attention determines the need for it. Parents may feel they give enough attention and may be correct by objective standards. The child may still feel a need because of the nature of the attention or the timing of it, or because of what she has to do to get it.

The need for general activity is another condition that is even harder to recognize and even more troublesome. "Doing nothing" usually leads to feeling a little depressed. Children do not easily know how to entertain themselves and parents often think they will naturally find something if told, "Go find something to do." Here's 7-year-old Joel and his dad:

Joel: "What a boring day!"
Dad: "Lousy weather." (See Chapter 1 about listening.)
Joel: "Yeah, It's too cold to do anything outside."
Dad: "Let's draw a plan for the garden."

Joel: "We don't need a plan now; that's way off."

Dad: "We could split it up, and you can have a part. Like this ..."

Joel's ability to busy himself got a little help from Dad today. He's not happy and bubbly about it, but the boredom will give way because Dad not only has an activity, he is letting Joel into it as an independent partner. Joel now has part of the garden.

Grumpy, bored, or depressed children or teens can often improve if they have a place to spend some energy. Adults learn this remedy for the blues early—exercise, chores, and projects.

Children often feel only an exciting and new activity will help—something wild like the experiences they see on TV. Most of us adults know that the remedy doesn't have to be that wild, which is good because "wild things" are rare. Dad will have to illustrate this advice many times as Joel picks up the habit.

If some structuring is not provided for the child who is at loose ends, he will cast about and over the undirected years come up with undesirable habits. How a child can entertain himself may be hard to discover if he has no responsibilities to fulfill, no opportunity for useful activity, and no reason to expect any benefit from his choices.

The search here is for a child's *opportunities*. It's not necessary to see that she always does it. Everyone has their own pace of living. But ongoing responsibilities should be available for even the younger children. Assigned chores, for example, provide something to do, something to be appreciated by others, something to be proud of, and something that is a source of self-esteem.

Some chores can be assigned (and rewarded) without specifying exactly when they are to be done. If you have a few jobs that you can do when the mood hits you, then that sudden urge for activity has somewhere to go and may occasionally be productive. Cleaning a room, practicing a musical instrument, vacuuming, working in the yard, and doing long-term homework assignments need support for their own sake as activities—not just for the result. So parental encouragement even for the unfinished project is important. If possible, let the child set the schedule and leave the nagging and badgering out.

EXERCISE
Fill In these important lists of priorities

Most of us find it easier to list the potential bad activities of our children and find it harder to think of the good ones. And the list of the bad tends to be more specific than the descriptions of good. "Don't go in the street," is specific enough to draw consequences when the child goes in the street. "Play safe" is too broad to be understood and too vague to draw much attention even if a child did it.

Keep this list handy in your notebook for sessions when one of these behaviors will be the subject of a new "behavior chart" from the exercise on page 67.

How would you describe your child's disposition? Give the evidence as you would if we were in court. What objective reasons would you give that the judge would accept, to support your statement that your child is say, "happy," "moody" or "playing safe?"

What priorities would you give to your lists of wanted and unwanted behaviors?

Viewed at the moment of aggravation, a child can seem to have acquired an unbearable habit. In writing down the complaint and prioritizing it, the description is often more objective. You may understand the problem better even before deciding what to do.

Try to include a behavior chart from the exercise on page 67 if you want to have a planning session about the problem. Does the problem usually happen when siblings are around, just before dinner or bedtime, or only when things are a bit boring? A little searching for the conditions may give you new ideas about the reasons for the problem.

What other behaviors of your child also seem to be a problem? We don't want to take on everything at once, but diverting your attention to other problems for a moment is helpful in deciding just how this complaint ranks in the larger picture. When the broad view is considered, the complaint might not get at the real problem and you might want to restate it. The complaint might be too trivial to worry about now. It doesn't have to be the most important problem in the family, but if it ends up too far down your list of important problems, you might want to choose a better priority.

Rejecting a problem as too unimportant is not wasted time. Some positive action can come of this discovery because often the initial problem was getting attention, reprimands, or nagging. Before moving on to a more important problem, you might want to consider inhibiting *all* corrections and comments for this low-priority problem. There is always the risk that part of the reason it exists at all is the attention it gets, and anyway the family airways can always use a little cleaning up to make room for more pleasant times. Now the behavior should cause you less irritation because you have put it in its place.

Try lists of both desired and undesired behaviors.

Chapter 4
Bad habits in childhood

Most parents are familiar with the dangers of childhood, if not the numbers. Football injuries top the list at 3800 injuries per million occasions of partici-pation. Soccer is next at 2400, then basketball at 1900 and cheerleading at 1700. Baseball causes 1400 injuries per million times the kids play the game and skateboarding scores a mere 800.

The numbers don't change much until the kids hit 15.

The S.A.D. behaviors:
Sex, alcohol, and drugs

In earlier generations the risks of sex, alcohol, and drugs were most frequently restricted to older teenagers. In these tough times, stories of the S.A.D. behaviors and sad consequences that reach even eight to 12-year-olds, show that accident and death rates are peaking earlier in each generation.

Parental habits can reduce the risk of S.A.D. behaviors.

The way you listen and teach and the role model you present, all influence risks in the dangerous business of growing up. The smothering wave of media hype and information will present all the possibilities of the abusive behaviors. Your listening can help straighten out the information; your observing and your liking can highlight the successes in following the right path; and your model can present the right direction.

It is hard for parents to keep up their effort because their influence shows itself gradually, usually without a child's dramatic announcement or abrupt change.

"Dad, do you drink?"

"I've had a beer on a hot day or maybe a wine sometimes at a party."

"How does it make you feel?"

"I don't drink enough to feel anything. I've learned it just makes me sleepy right away and sick later."

"Can I try it?"

"When you're older."

I think most of us parents would feel uncomfortable in this conversation. We are in the dangerous area of hypocrisy and not much progress is being made. As far as extracting a guarantee of abstinence from a child, we may feel impatient with Dad. But in building an attitude, a little progress on the big job may have been accomplished.

The topic is so dangerous that the necessary long talks themselves seem dangerous. When our own shortcomings are dragged out for review, the temptation is to fall back on lecturing. The lecture will be an attempt to extract a promise of abstinence, but the only guarantee of safe behavior is in the long term of establishing values. I would give this Dad high marks for keeping his eye on that goal.

Listening is critical in the discussions of dangerous behaviors. A feeling of confidence and self-esteem, as overworked as those terms are in child-rearing, are the best protection parents have to offer a child today.

> **Listening is critical in discussions of dangerous behaviors.**

I'm not going to have a drink for lunch today, nor drugs this afternoon, or dangerous, life-threatening sex tonight. The statistics would say you will probably avoid the same things. Why? Because we both feel we have too much to lose. We have family and work responsibilities and goals we have set for ourselves. We hope to make a contribution to our community and family and have some success in our jobs. Too much to lose—that's how we see ourselves.

Who will point out what wonderful talents and potentials this child has to lose? My conversation with a drug-experimenting pre-teen is tragically typical:

"So let me get this all straight," I say. "You took some white powder your friend had in his garage, put it on a piece of glass in a little row. Then you took a straw and smiffed it up your nose?"

"Well, yeah."

"What about the dirt, let alone the stuff itself. How could you be sure it was clean or even made of what he said it was?"

"Well, I didn't know, but I figure, you know, what have I got to lose?"

(My parent outrage almost pops out.) "What have you got to lose!? You've got your whole life ahead..."

I know what I have to lose, why doesn't this kid know what *he* has to lose? All those lectures in school—about health, brain damage, infection, addiction, and the violence of the people involved in this trade—and he still can ask, "What do I have to lose?" The lectures are to groups, of course, and they leave out the personal abilities, individual prospects, and talents. Who will tell our sons and daughters what they, personally, have to lose?

How does a child learn to value himself, learn what he has to lose? That self-respect will come from developing competencies—even everyday ones like cooking, keeping track of money, and doing domestic chores.

One boy said to me that he told his friends he couldn't cruise the mall because, "I make dinner on Tuesdays and I already bought the stuff." There's a small step in the direction of self-confidence.

So one of the best protections against dangerous behaviors is the parental habit of providing satisfying tasks that build confidence.

The concern about sex, alcohol, and drugs also requires strategies focusing on learning what is going on. The effects of experimental drug-taking, for example, are the same symptoms parents see everyday. Cold-like symptoms, changes in sleeping and eating patterns, new friends, new attitudes, new demands about money, longer hours at the mall, and hanging out. All very normal unless they all happen at once.

It's the clustering that should alert you. When the hangout, the mall or corner, suddenly takes much more time, the sniffles become an annoyance to the whole family, demands for new curfew hours increase, and money is suddenly missing, or suddenly acquired and cannot be explained, it's time to be suspicious.

Battery-operated security blankets

Mom says, "Put down that gadget and talk with your aunt. She's only visiting for today." Techy teen looks up and answers a few questions, but he doesn't release his grip around his game and the lifeline to his friends. That battery-operated social security wire is often a social lifeline as well.

You would think this would be a problem of children and the not-quite adults. But if you include TV watching, the 45-and-over age group is the most addicted with 1,000 hours per year devoted to the little and big screens. That's forty 24-hour days of watching per year. Teenagers watch about 30 days per year.

Among those parents who play video games, the average age of video gamers is 34. One fourth of them are over 50. Among parents of teens, 48 percent play video games with their kids one or more times each week.

Among teenagers, the amount of socializing (talking) without hand-held assistance, is about the same as in previous, non-electronic, generations. So the total amount of communication between teens, bolstered by the battery-operated chit-chat, is way up compared to years ago. We hope something good comes of that.

The electronics are here to stay and 21st century parents will have to share the family air-time with yet another intrusion from the exploding electronic lifestyle.

Check your conversational style, the one without a keyboard, I mean. The competition for a free moment is getting harder. Parents who have retained the most influence with their kids are still the ones with good listening skills.

They put down their distractions and turn off all hand-helds when a chance to talk with their child-teen comes up.

They show the good body language of paying attention: they look at their teen, they turn toward him, and keep frequent eye contact.

They avoid the temptation to "get in their licks." They know the kids wonder first, "What does this talk say about ME?"

They understand that the greatest fear among most teens is embarrassment. To keep the defensiveness less likely, they use "it" and "others" to keep the conversation less personal—not "you" and not "me."

They know the conversation does not have to declare a winner or find the blame. Most conversations need no conclusion and no summing up.

With these tools at the ready, the duel between Ipod-laptop worship and just talking with Mom and Dad will come out more even.

Twitter, Facebook, blogs, emails and computer games can be the most problematic time-stealers when the kids have time on their hands. It is difficult to monitor and control the electric idols.

Mom and Dad have to look over a kid's shoulder to assess these activities because we have no useful ratings for these intruders into family time.

"No electronics before lunch" might be a good summer rule and "No electronics during or after supper" could be the school year routine that allows more quality family conversation.

Of course you have to be a good model for these rules, so set your limits carefully. Be sure you can obey your own rules.

In setting these standards, we can all benefit from the advice of fellow parents to sort out the good from the bad and the ugly. Here's where a Parent Support Group can be a pool of information exchange and discussion.

Not only can a group help evaluate movies and electronics, it can be a source of comfort and satisfaction to know that others have problems similar to yours.

> **Be sure you can obey your own rules.**

Among the 80 percent of teens who have embraced hand-held technology, 75 percent have unlimited texting using a family contract. Only 10 percent have their own contract, reports the Pew Research Center.

Ninety-eight percent of their parents say texting helps teenagers "keep in touch." All of this has happened in the last five years; my version of Word software underlines "texting" in red as a spelling error.

Pew Research says 30 percent of teens send over 100 messages each day; only 22 percent send less than 10 messages per day.

Before you conclude that staring at little screens and using a keyboard the size of a postage stamp is all bad, consider these other habits. Cell phone, land line and face-to-face communication with friends have NOT gone down. Texting and twittering have only added to the social networking of teens. Taken all together such social skill exercise has almost doubled since the hand-held gadgets became popular.

Kids entering this technological swirl of flying messages bring with them already established habits with phones, cell phones and just one-on-one talking. As another school year starts, stories start trickling home about school and life from 10- to 18-year-olds in the teenage stress-lane. Since parents are usually not frequent texters, parent-talk on serious topics often occurs in the old-fashioned way—face-to-face.

Now is a good time for parents to review their listening habits. Face-to-face conversation has many advantages. Your body language shows through, your eye contact confirms you hear the other person, and you can model a quiet and respectful tone not possible with a little gadget.

The trick for parents is to keep the flood of shocked reactions in check and yet remain a good listener. Parents often say to me, "He takes things so personally." So first of all, keep the subject on a third person basis as much as possible as you would with an adult.

Teen: "What a crummy math teacher."

Mom: "Hard to get that stuff the first time." Mom sides with her son by not falling into an argument (you shouldn't talk about your teachers like that). She just reflects the same feeling, but says nothing new while waiting for more information.

Keep these listening skills handy. Adults are very good talkers without any kind of keypad. We have decades of practice, but our children, even practiced networking teenagers, have less experience and may fall back on defense if challenged with regular talking.

A parent-child (or teen) "talking ritual" can help parents keep up with how it's going and give extra practice with conversation.

Without the habit of talking with Mom and Dad, your student is likely to seek a "second family." Peers, iPods, text messages, and Internet information can all substitute for real parent role models.

The "boy problem"

Boys are five times more likely than girls to have accidents with bikes, sticks, and baseball bats. Later on, they are four times more likely to have trouble with the law. They cause most teen driving accidents and get most of the traffic tickets. They also have lower grades in school and are more likely to drop out. Boys have shrunk to a minority in colleges, medical schools, and law schools. Although girls were rarely allowed in these institutions a century ago, now, for every 100 male college graduates there are over 140 women graduates

> **Boys have shrunk to a minority in colleges, medical schools, and law schools.**

By 12th grade, 44 percent of girls have become proficient readers but only 28 percent of boys have reached that standard. Only 41 percent of boys said they "often" tried to do their best work in school, compared with 67 percent of the girls.

Now that the "male chores" of the farm have become less needed in city life, girls have an advantage. Girls make an earlier contribution to the family, particularly in the domestic chores. As a result, they enjoy early appreciation and are better prepared to care for themselves.

One boy came to me to sign out of college. "Sorry you are leaving," I said.

"I just can't handle all the problems."

"What problems?"

"Little things. For example, I can't get my laundry done."

"Why not?"

"Well, I went down to our laundry room, and there were all these cycles and settings. Even my underwear came out pink."

"You could throw the laundry away and buy new stuff," I said, but added, "I was just joking," when I saw his tears of frustration welling up.

"I know, but I couldn't buy stuff. I don't know my size!"

He was dropping out of his first year of college partly because the number on the elastic of his underpants followed his tail around all his life but was only read by Mom. After a childhood with no practice, he couldn't handle college life.

Dads are particularly vulnerable to falling down on the job of providing support for practice in daily chores. Dads can also easily fall into competition with their sons and hold back on compliments for chores well done for fear of appearing weak. As a result, dozens of young men have told me, "As far as my Dad was concerned, I always felt I was a little short of his expectations."

One 17-year-old told me that after she told her father her senior grades, all A's and a "B" in math, her father said, "Why didn't you come to me? You know I have always been good in math."

Another student of mine told me that when he took up the saxophone on his own he didn't tell his dad because he knew he would only hear criticism. When he finally told his father he won a high school contest in music, his father said, "Well, music has always been easy for you."

So support your school's active projects in home improvement, financial management, small business management, mortgages, stock markets, computer management, applied science, and tracking diet and exercise. These projects encourage both boys and girls to be proud of their abilities right now. Even abstract subjects can include practical projects even though college applications won't ask about "non-academic" skills.

Schoolwork should help your son with his concerns now, at his present age. "Someday you'll need this," is not enough.

Going from father to grandfather, I went from girls who have the highest grades in school and are the least likely to need school discipline, to boys who are most likely to be disciplined and six times more likely to have trouble with the law, with driving, with alcohol and drugs. They are also six times more likely to go to prison later on.

Is all this genetic? Some of it must be. But there are positive and negative contributing factors from parents and grandparents.

Many parents, teachers, and counselors believe girls are more socially skilled at an earlier age and therefore may attract more support, acceptance, and admiration than their brothers. Boys on the other hand, seem to want only to be competent and admired for it. They seem to shun the gushier praise.

Parents shouldn't be misled by a son's bland reaction. To prove they are not easily influenced, boys often fend off sincere praise in the years when they need it most.

The lack of enthusiasm from a son may lead parents to conclude that compliments and admiration don't work, so they should lay off the positive approach of compliments and encouragement. This is a deadly mistake.

Parents should not be misled by short-term rebuffs because the long-term results are more important. The temptation to let boys go their own way, with discipline for only the big blunders and a trickle of support for the successes, is destructive to skill development in boys.

Dads are particularly vulnerable to taking up this strategy and come off looking as if they never completely approve of anything their son does.

A strange effect of sexism in our culture is that girls sometimes show better adjustment in childhood than boys because they make an earlier contribution to the family, particularly in the domestic chores. They enjoy early appreciation and are encouraged to do more.

While "protecting" a boy from drudgery, parents can run the risk of driving their son to find other activities that show he can "do something."

Threatened by his perceived "worthlessness," he will cast around for a way to show off—what will he find? Will it be a suggestion from his Mom or Dad? Or will urging from friends who encourage risky behaviors take over?

Positive support is the major advantage parents have in competing against their child's friends who encourage and criticize without much thought. Parents have to hold to limits that are not always popular, but also must inspire new tasks that build self-respect.

One fast way to alienate a member from a group (or family) is to deny him a chance to contribute when he's ready. Gripe as he may about chore assignments and household jobs, recognition of his steps forward now will help maintain his genuine satisfaction with himself later on when peers encourage dangerous habits.

The driving threat

The biggest danger to children, bigger than all childhood diseases and accidents, comes when they are almost grown. In the late teenage years, emergency room visits jump from 30 to 60 per million per day, and the death rate skyrockets from one per million per day to 10!

The big change is, of course, driving.

A survey by the Liberty Mutual Insurance Company and Students Against Destructive Decisions interviewed over 1,300 teen drivers with accidents or recent near misses. All parents should know the survey results these dedicated students reported after interviewing their fellow drivers.

Over 68 percent of these teens who have had traffic incidents said they were distracted at the crucial moment (47 percent had more than two passengers with them). Sixty-one percent were changing songs on the screen of a portable player. And 36 percent said they were texting when the accident or near miss occurred. The same proportion said they were on their cell phone. Forty-six percent admitted they were speeding.

> **Over 68 percent of teens who have had traffic incidents said they were distracted at the crucial moment.**

The driving hours these multi-taskers reported increased in the summer.

In July and August these teens averaged 28.6 driving hours per week. In the school year they averaged 16.4 hours. Still only seven percent said summer driving was more dangerous.

Using car seats and seat belts works well for young children, but when they turn 16, all parental efforts are overwhelmed and swept aside by the shocking statistics of driving and riding with reckless friends.

Girls are now almost as much at risk as boys. In 1990, 160 of every 1000 under-18 girls wrecked their cars that year and by 2000 the number was 175. The boys are steady at 210 per 1000 per year.

Alcohol abuse plays a large role. The National Center on Addiction and Substance Abuse reports that girls drink just as much as boys—48 percent of girls drink; 52 percent of boys. In 2000, among high school freshmen, girls nudged out the boys for first place in reports of regular drinking—41 percent of girls and 40 percent of boys.

This summer will bring another round of deaths from drunk and risky driving. You don't want to wake up in the middle of the night to that terrible phone call, "This is Officer Smith of the State Police, Your daughter (son) has been . . ."

Parents who get that call will pray, in that first heart-stopping instant, that it only involves an arrest or accident and not an injury or death.

The statistics would say Mom and Dad probably gave permission for the driving plan after extracting a few promises—no deviations from the plan, no craziness, and, they might have said no drinking—but all were likely violated at the fatal moment with the tragic result.

Saying, "Be careful" is not enough. Limitations and restrictions need to be enforced. Better yet, join a parent team that will check on your teen's friends and their evening plans in exchange for your promise to check on yours.

Nothing else you have ever done to protect them during all their growing up years is as important as your riding and driving rules.

The bad movie problem

Often when a parent hears "But Mom, all the kids are going," it concerns going to a movie with questionable values. The high-tech and low entertainment of many films aimed at kids puts parents in a position of judging movies they have not seen and don't want to see. You can't rely on the ratings because many of the ratings presume you will see the movies (Parental Discretion Advised). This is a ludicrous presumption for parents with children under 13. They really think parents will review the movie and then provide informed parental guidance when the children react to the hype? Dedicated parents, the industry evidently feels, should set aside say, six hours a week to carry out this responsibility although the TV and Hollywood producers think it is too financially risky to address.

> **Parents need to make sure their perspective is part of the movie discussion.**

The struggle between parent and child over "media control" often starts with those PG-13 and R-rated movies. Since you can't trust the film makers, you are left with the ratings or checking out every movie that comes along. Since no parent has that much time, a movie-by-movie decision is very hard to do. Many parents tell me they avoid most (not all) of the arguing by using a rule about ratings instead of individual movies: PG-13 movies only after parents have learned about the movie; No R-rated movies.

For the older kids, you could drop the restriction on the PG-13 movies, but as we all know, it's the values presented that parents need to consider. If you spend all week telling your child how to act toward others, it's not productive to follow that up with a PG-13 movie that has four mindless killings, presents parents and other adults as dolts, solves problems in 27 minutes, and shows money as the root of all happiness!

So PG-13 movies have to be watched carefully for the values they espouse. They can have a story that shows growth and good sense, but often the plot revolves around a smart but naive girl and a street-wise but good-hearted rascal who suspect a crime. The mandatory features seem to be a straight, somewhat stupid parent figure, teacher, or police chief, a villain who thinks kids are just inconveniences, a car chase and/or a director's favorite: helicopters! At least one spectacular explosion is mandatory along with some bad language and an implication of romance and/or sex (this is where the "PG-13" comes in).

> **Parents need to consider the values presented.**

The PG-13's can also send dangerous messages about violence. They often include a lot of hitting that has great effect but does little damage (very few open cuts, bruises or long hospital stays—not a good perspective for a child to develop). Messages about shooting show misses (that go "zingggg") and hits that result in instant death for minor characters or a confession or "heavy" remark for exit of major characters.

In the end the villain gets his/her comeuppance and parent figures realize just how wise this girl and street-wise rascal really are. Girl and Rascal are heroes and probably never have to go to school again.

R (rarely acceptable for children) movies.

Many R-rated movies treat important themes and are good learning experiences and entertainment for children who are ready to understand them. Most young children are not ready for the adult topics and, in the adult girl-and-rascal plot, they will only remember that sex was glorified, violence was intensified, and the language was terrible.

Movies, TV, music, computers, talk shows, and the Internet all need careful attention for the messages they send. The media can provide a positive advantage as a starting point for productive conversations on sensitive topics if good listening habits become routine. Parents need to make sure their adult perspective is part of the discussion.

Since children and teens are a lucrative marketing segment, film and TV producers have a stake in pandering to the values (or lack of them) and the self-interest of this market. Add to this the common ploy of glorifying children and teens while ridiculing authority figures and you can see that now, more than ever, you need to keep your adult perspective and guide your children to healthier ways of spending their time.

Here's where a Parent Support Group can be a pool of information exchange and discussion. Not only can a group help evaluate movies and electronics, it can be a source of comfort and satisfaction to know that others have problems similar to yours.

When should your child start smoking?

I haven't seen any plans for tobacco companies to go out of business, so I guess they are counting on somebody's children to fill in for smokers who die.

Each day 3,000 American teenagers under 18 begin daily smoking, but if your child delays joining the ranks, there are good consequences. For example, two teeth. Yes, smokers lose, on the average, two more teeth each decade than nonsmokers. So just delaying smoking from eight until 18 saves two teeth! Of course another 12 teeth are goners in the decades between 18 and 78.

> **Young smokers have twice the likelihood of colds, flu, and respiratory disorders each year.**

If your children delay smoking until 20, then, in addition to saving two teeth, they are likely to delay turning prematurely gray as well, since smokers are four times more likely to turn gray prematurely. Also delaying smoking will put off balding since men who smoke are twice as likely to be bald or balding as non-smoking men.

In the long term, smokers have thinner, less elastic skin which means more wrinkles than nonsmokers. So children who wait until 25 to start smoking will look ten years younger at age 50 than classmates who started smoking at 15. I guess that's an advantage.

But starting young has other consequences. For example, young smokers have twice the likelihood of colds, flu, and respiratory disorders each year. Young smokers are also much more likely to try marijuana, and teens who have tried marijuana are twice as likely to try other drugs.

If your child delays smoking until 30, other statistics kick in. First, he or she is likely to forget to start smoking at all (more than 80 percent of starters begin in high school, 90 percent before 21).

So when should your child start smoking? Later is better, but never is better than late.

Actually, the percentage of young people starting to smoke hasn't changed much over the decades. But the increasing number of quitters has gone up resulting in an overall decrease in adult smokers from almost 80 percent in 1948 to 44 percent in 1964, to 29 percent in 1987, and less than 27 percent today.

For all those ex-smokers, the health and longevity benefits start coming right away.

After 20 minutes without smoking, blood pressure decreases, pulse rate drops, body temperature of hands and feet increases.

Eight hours after quitting, carbon monoxide levels in the blood drop to normal and the oxygen level increases to normal. After 24 hours the chance of a heart attack decreases. After two weeks circulation improves and walking is easier.

At one year, the excess risk of heart disease is decreased to half that of a regular smoker. Five years and stroke risk is down to that of a non-smoker. Ten years and lung cancer risk is down by half. Fifteen years and risk of heart disease and death rate are reduced to that of non-smokers.

Mom's and Dad's smoking habits are the biggest factor in children delaying smoking or never starting at all. Over 60 percent of smokers under age 19 are children of parents who smoke (70 percent for girls and 54 percent of boys). Only 35 percent of the smokers under 19 are children of nonsmokers.

So after all the arguing about smoking statistics, what's the best thing a smoking parent can do to steer the kids in the right direction?
Quit.

Battle of the bulge

Obesity is an unpleasant word reserved for body fat that's out of control.

For children, obesity is reached when total body weight is more than 25 percent fat for boys, 32 percent for girls. Normally, two out of ten children are in this category, but the number can reach eight out of ten if both parents are obese.

In 1970 we fed ourselves on 3,300 calories each day. That was the production consumed from food companies in the USA in those days. Now we are up to 3,800 calories a day according to Marion Nestle's book, *Food Politics: How the Food Industry Influences Nutrition and Health*.

The extra 500 daily calories (equivalent to an extra banana split every day) has added 10 pounds to the average weight of a teenager compared with kids of the 90s, says the Pediatricians Research Group of Woodlands, TX. It's not surprising when you consider we tempt ourselves with over 10,000 new food products each year—mostly candy, snacks, soft drinks, baked goods, and ice creams.

Of course exercise enters in. Teenagers who report more than five hours of sedentary TV per day are five times more likely to be overweight than kids watching less than two hours each day. Snacks during TV, say, a small bag of potato chips each day, will add a half pound each week. Not much you might think, but it totals up to a 26-pound weight-gain each year.

The weight problem of our children is bulging about as fast as their parents' poundage. Back in 1991, when we were each consuming not much more than 3,300 calories per day, only Mississippi, Alabama, and West Virginia had more than 15 percent obese adults. Now more than 20 percent of adults are obese in over half the states.

No doubt the food pushers both at home and in the food business deserve some of the blame for the increases. TV with too many commercials about food and computer time with too much junk food handy are bad routines.

Parents can set a slow pace at family meals, even when eating out as much as Americans do. Serving sizes in restaurants are ever larger and parents should keep limits in place even there. The kids could take a doggy bag home, too.

At home, serving water at every meal and having everyone serve their plates, then putting the extra away before sitting down, are healthy habits.

Everything we do requires some effort and inconvenience. All behaviors, even getting out the donuts or hot snack, have an inconvenience. You have to get a plate, find a fork, warm it up, get a drink to go with it.

So keep the healthy food handy and ready—fruit on the table, ice water instead of soft drinks in the fridge. Let the fat, salt, and sugar be the ones that are the most trouble to get from the store and the most troublesome to get out at home. The kids will buy other snacks, but at least at home your diet and their's will be better.

Mom, I think I have a problem

We all hope this problem turns out to be simple and not too serious—maybe a tough homework assignment or a fellow student with bad social skills. We hope it is not the forever life-changing announcement. But you might have a moment of fear if you have heard the statistics of teenage pregnancies.

How should a parent talk to his or her teen about this sensitive subject? Avoiding the topic and withholding information will not postpone the risks. "If I don't know how to do it safely, I won't do it," is not a popular teenage motto.

A conversation too short, too fast, or with too many family members chiming in is not likely to help. Pick a good time when you can go slow with time to listen in a one-on-one situation.

Make sure your teen gets the facts straight. One teenaged girl told me, "I want to be safe. If I have sex, I always sneak one of Mom's pills the next day." In the United States, daughters have a 1 in 20 chance of becoming pregnant, and both sons and daughters are at three times that risk for sexually transmitted diseases. This is not just a "girl problem."

Before you talk with your teen, a little self-inspection is in order. What do you want to say to your son about his responsibilities in a relationship? What message does he get in the non-serious moments about his (and his Dad's) attitude toward women and sex? What do you want to say about contraceptives? Abortion? At what age do you want to bring these topics up?

The fathers who cause high school teen pregnancies are usually long out of high school themselves, so caution your teenage daughter about these "older kids" and talk to your 17-and-something son about this temptation.

Alcohol is the most common excuse young women give for making the big mistake. What attitudes should a parent model on this subject?

When it's time to get serious, remember all those listening skills. Keep your pace of conversation slow. Reserve your answers and advice until your teen has a chance to express his/her opinion. Before you give all your guidance, you need to learn what they know, or think they know.

Remember that one session on this topic will not be enough, so conclusions with "You should...," "Don't ever...," and "Be careful not to..." don't have to be said in the first conversation. Take your time, it may be the most important part of your influence on your son's or daughter's future.

Who's to blame?

Teenager bashing has been a favorite pastime as far back as history goes. From Socrates of ancient Greece, who complained about disrespectful teenagers, to 90's President Clinton's proposals blaming guns in schools, teenagers seem to be a long-standing whipping post. But when the numbers are considered, you get a different picture.

President Clinton was right to worry about gun violence in our culture, but he got the age wrong when he singled out murders by "13-year-olds with automatic weapons" as the top priority. Actually FBI reports show it's the 47-year-olds (Clinton's age at the time) who are twice as likely to commit murder as 13-year-olds. In fact, 83 percent of murdered children, 85 percent of murdered adults, and over half the murdered teenagers are killed by adults over 20.

> **What attitudes should an adult model?**

Even respected organizations exaggerate the statistics bashing teens. The American Medical Association reports "half a million" unmarried teenagers become pregnant each year (the actual number is about 280,000). They also claim a "30-fold" increase in teenage crime since 1950, but comprehensive national reports show no increase at all in the last two decades.

Also, overall teen drug and alcohol use has remained constant or decreased over the last 15 years. For example, the percent of high school seniors who report using cocaine within the last 12 months is down from 12 percent in 1984 to 5 percent in 2000—not good, but better. Certainly drug education programs for teens deserve much of the credit for these promising trends.

On the adult side, the statistics are grim. Federal crime statistics show federal drug offenses (almost all adults) up from 12,000 in the 1980's to 23,000 by 1999, almost doubled and still climbing.

Of course, support of programs for teens is money well spent. But when teens are also blamed as the cause, it lets us adults off the hook.

Articles about bad teens usually blame, first of all, teen depravity made worse by rap music, gangs, and lenient courts. Mentioned later on or not at all are causes that are too expensive for the well-paid men and women of Congress: poverty, racial injustice, unemployment, and bad schools.

In fact, for every act of violence or sexual offense committed by a person under 18, three such crimes are committed by adults against children and teens. Here's the topper: the 1992 report of the National Victims Center found that of 12 million women raped that year, two-thirds were raped before they were 18, the average age being 11. But the average age of their attackers was 27!

The notion that teenage pregnancy is entirely the fault of the kids is also inaccurate. Men over 20 cause nearly 90 percent of the pregnancies among junior-high girls and 70 percent of the high school pregnancies. This is not "children having children;" this is adults abusing children.

Those who favor condom distribution and those who would instead demand abstinence education shouldn't be fooled into thinking that it's only young boys with young girls who cause the trouble. Even if their good efforts resulted in every high school boy abstaining from sex as conservatives would like or using a condom as others have proposed, most "teen pregnancies" would still happen, because, most often, it is an adult man who is the father.

As the comic strip character, Pogo, so rightly said, "We have met the enemy and he is us."

The *New York Times* has reported that the introduction of the pill in the 50's did not reduce dangerous sexual habits as was first predicted. National rates of teen pregnancies, births, and abortions did not peak in the 50's but continued upward until the 90's. Even now many states average 60 unmarried teenage girls per week who have babies.

> **Men over 20 cause nearly 90 percent of the pregnancies among junior-high girls and 70 percent of the high school pregnancies.**

The pregnancy rate is actually higher than that because many pregnancies end before they are reported, and aborted pregnancies (about one third) are not included.

Speaking of unwanted pregnancies reminds us that the pill was approved by the Food and Drug Administration 50 years ago (1960). Few of the pill's promoters imagined how the pill would become a powerful tool for transforming women's lives.

In the *New York Times* report, reporter Elaine Tyler May said, "Today, women no longer need to choose between having a family and a career. At the pill's 50th anniversary, that alone is well worth celebrating."

Values learned through the family connections

The values a child acquires come partly through the family connections. Parents pass their values along in their reactions about what they approve and disapprove, and their values are recycled through the family. So while a baby reacts to only what it needs and a toddler has learned some practical strategies for satisfying those needs, an older child forms opinions of right and wrong. The nature of the parental signals and consequences determines how suitable and appropriate these opinions turn out to be.

How do values change? Theories that take on this question suggest several sources beyond parental influence. They maintain that values grow from experience and inborn inclinations as well as the values of the community, extended family, church, and religious influence.

Most of the theories concerning the mysteries of children have a thread of truth to them. All parents have recognized a little heredity in the actions of their children, watched them learn from experience, and have seen the effects of early crucial experiences both positive and traumatic. But while all these explanations are genuine parts of child psychology and can help us understand how a child's values develop, not all explanations point to sources that parents can influence. So while a child's heritage and past experiences are influential, they cannot be changed. But now and in the future, parents can express their own values in talking with their children. Your influence is in your actions and your present conversation.

> **Parental values will be passed along in the daily interactions.**

Parental values will be passed along in the daily interactions, but the influence of everyday family interactions may be hard to recognize in children. The permanent genetics and semi-constant "disposition" and "personality" of a child are easier to see, and they can make parents pessimistic about their own effect.

What can a parent do, for example, when told that her daughter is "not considerate of others," "shows no interest in schoolwork," or is "lacking in social skills?" By themselves, these descriptions that reflect values suggest nothing specific except, "Maybe she should try a little harder." Her mother might be told "she will grow out of it" or that nothing can be done because we assume she was born that way, without interest in school or other people.

But to say that nothing can be done is unrealistic because *something will be done* the next time she acts inconsiderate, uninterested, or makes another social blunder. Mom or her teacher or playmates will react in some way. Even ignoring the problem is a reaction that has an effect.

So in spite of the way they were born or conditioned, children make adjustments to the reactions of their parents as best they can, and parents adjust as best they can. One mother turned from a backyard talk with me to deal with her son, Brian, who was screaming.

"Mommy! Mommy! Mommy!"

Finally she yelled back, "All right! What is it?!"

He said, "Hi" and ran away smiling.

She knew she had rewarded his nonsense with attention he didn't deserve, and she had also given him an additional example of yelling herself, but what was she to do? She turned back to me and shrugged, "Boys will be boys."

Yes, he was born a boy and that may have something to do with the yelling, but the explanation shouldn't be used to excuse his behavior nor should it excuse Mom from trying a new way to make things better. Perhaps he should have been ignored—painful as that might have been. Perhaps she should have used the "that's one" approach. Whatever solution Mom tries, she needs to become a shrewd observer. When she knows what Brian is doing and why, the decision concerning reactions is easier.

What are the useful explanations of behavior? For the ages beyond two, explanations of even simple behaviors can be numerous. We need one consistent plan of action that pinpoints the behavior and provides reactions that are appropriate. Careful observation may show that acting "inconsiderate," "tired," or "messy," can be sorted out by the time of day and a few questions. Parents can ask each other about how the problem developed, or, in the case of school work, they can ask the *child* questions about school that would tell them if a problem has been frustrating or homework is dreaded.

> **Parents need one consistent plan of action that pinpoints the behavior and provides reactions that are appropriate.**

Armed with more information from listening well, both Dad and Mom can react constructively when the conflicts over the values of daily routines come up: messy mealtime behavior will result in the messed-up food being taken away for a time, or a rule that says: homework must be done before dinner.

Enforcing such rules without exceptions isn't going to create a happy home. But a lack of *any* thoughtful planning is going to leave the child confused at first, and then, with practice, the child will learn to manipulate the outcomes by "acting angry" or "acting tired" when it promises to be to his advantage.

The worst outcome from lack of focus on specifics and planned reactions is that the parents will disagree and be driven apart. They have their own stake in what happens in each situation and need time together to plan cooperative reactions. Differences in values about daily chores and entertainment will not confuse a child for long. When treated with honesty, differences between parents can be tolerated.

Long-term disagreements about standards will create new strategies in the kids playing one parent against the other. In the confusion, the child gains too much control with a "divide and conquer" strategy.

With practice, a child will deal with the variations in human attitudes. But in the long-term conflicts he can discover strategies to deal with unreliable parental habits and the whole interaction can become very dissatisfying and eventually downright destructive to the family.

Values have not always been a popular subject in child-rearing. We have often viewed children as easily swayed from whatever values they may hold. A "good talking to," a reprimand, and a correction will set it all straight. The approach assumes that "outside events" will change the inside feelings. Some psychologists believe that because "inside events" such as mental processes, emotions, and values cannot be seen, we should focus on the observable outside events—the behaviors and the reactions to them: what the child does to the world and what the world does to the child in return.

When behaviors were bad, "behaviorists" examined them not as symptoms of deeper unreachable problems but as the result of other outside events, the experiences of the child. Obviously there are disadvantages to a rigid behaviorist's point of view. Children certainly do have an interior life of feelings, emotions, fears, and joys. Without a consideration of these real events, a great deal of understanding of how children behave would be lost.

But an approach that is too theoretical can also be dangerous because it tempts us adults to blame it all on what's going on inside the child (he's rebellious) and we can become overwhelmed by how complex it all seems (she's at a bad age). If we conclude that nothing can be done because of conditions inside, we will be no help to the child.

The dangers of inside blames

Credits and blames direct the evaluation of ideas to the person. "Why would *you* think of that? That shows *you* are to blame, wrong, or off-base." Once the score card is part of the conversation, the tallies get more attention than the ideas.

We can recognize good points in a conversation, but for the wrong or misguided remarks we distribute the blame for our errors and those of others differently. For *our own* mistakes we usually choose "outside blame" that says we are unfortunate and misled victims. "I had to lie; it's a dog-eat-dog world out there!" "Outside blame" for our own mistakes extends to other people, "I was late because people drive so slow!"

When it comes to the mistakes of *others* (including children), whether in values or in action, we are tempted to use "inside blame." "What (inside condition) makes him so inconsiderate, so clumsy? Why doesn't she pay more attention? What was she thinking of?"

Inside blame is a dangerous habit. Parents should use it carefully. It leads to frustration and inaction because the child is viewed as "having" (inside) a nearly unchangeable character.

Outside blame leads parents to look for problem *situations* instead of problem *children*. With a good understanding of a problem situation, we have a chance to discover a workable solution. That, in turn, gives the child a new chance.

> **Outside blame leads parents to look for problem situations rather than problem children and offers a better chance for a solution.**

In order to plan reactions to problem situations, you need a clear view of what's happening. Blaming the child doesn't help because it's too vague and it makes assumptions about what is going on inside the child. For example, in the complaint that Dylan is "too demanding and selfish," Mom may have real actions of Dylan in mind, but she also implies that his demands are intentional and unreasonable. The result is that the blame has been put inside Dylan, and Dylan's parents are likely to look for the cure there.

Dylan: "Daddy! Daddy!"
Dad: "Just a minute, Dylan, I'm listening to your mother."
Dylan: "Daddy!"
Dad: "Just a minute!"

Dylan: "Daddy, I need to go to the *bathroom!*"
Dad: "What? OK. (turning to Mom) I'll take him."
Dylan: "I don't need to."
Dad: "You just said ..."
Dylan: "I mean, I don't need any help."
Dad: "Well, just go ahead and go!"
Dylan: (From the bathroom) "Daddy, I need help."
Dad: "I'll be right there."
Dylan: "I'm washing my hands!"
Dad: "So you *didn't* need help!" (Walks back to Mom) "He's so selfish! He wants our attention all the time."
Mom: "Maybe we should forget the selfish part and try to give him more attention for other things."
Dylan: "Daddy!"
Dad: (Almost losing it) "What!?"
Dylan: "I went to the bathroom...by myself."
Dad: (A little tired) "Good, Dylan."

Instead of fixing the blame (he's selfish), Mom suggested they look for the reactions from the *outside* world that Dylan gets for being so demanding. It could be that attention for acting selfish is Dylan's game. Even an argument between Mom and Dad about his demanding nature could be rewarding. The "Why?" of behavior is again best answered by changing "Why?" to "What happens next?"

Dylan makes a demand and then what happens? And, when Dylan behaves in non-demanding ways, what happens then? An answer to this question about reactions to Dylan's good behavior will be useful. This outside focus will lead to a plan to support Dylan and to exercise caution in reacting to mistakes. Later, when Dylan is having one of his rare moments when he has no demand, the conversation could start:

Dad: "Dylan, tell me about this picture you drew."
(Message: You don't have to act up or make demands to get Dad's attention.)

Useful "blames" (explanations) will not be found in the basic character of Dylan nor in the basic character of Dylan's parents! The useful answer is most likely found in the common give-and-take between Dylan and his family surroundings. Here's a different example:

Amanda: "I got my room cleaned up."
Dad: "Great!"
Amanda: "I didn't pick up my blocks because I'm not finished with the fire station I'm building with them."

Here's a crucial moment for Dad. His choices are: continue support for what was done—after all, half a loaf is better than none, or hold out for a higher standard and only give credit when the whole job is done.

A definition of what is acceptable would help. Doesn't Amanda have the option of leaving one ongoing project out? Amanda's parents will have to make this judgment regarding Amanda's progress and potential, but the parental habit here should be to err on the side of support—an overdose in support is not a great danger in child-rearing.

Another concern for Dad is what kind of credit he should give. "Outside credit" may be "no credit" at all for Amanda: "I guess the mess finally got to you. Even *you* couldn't stand it any more." So Dad shouldn't give the credit to Amanda's environment for driving her to do the right thing, and he shouldn't take the credit himself by saying, "Well now, didn't *I* tell you that would be better?" Dad should give the credit directly to Amanda for getting the job done:

> **Parents should err on the side of support; an overdose of support is not a great danger in child-rearing.**

Dad: "Well, you still need the blocks out; you would have to just about wreck your firehouse to put it away. *You* (not me and not your surroundings) have it looking good in here."

Family confusions about blames.

Recognizing the priorities of needs can sometimes explain the otherwise puzzling fate of some rules. For example, I worked with two very different sisters whose reactions to cleaning up their rooms were very confusing.

Dawn needed to be constantly assured that her parents thought she was capable and successful, and she tried hard to be cooperative and helpful. Her sister, Kim, also seemed to value her parents' approval but wanted prolonged attention and companionship more than praise.

A rule that reminded their mother to praise both daughters for keeping their room nice worked well for Dawn seeking praise. But since attention ended when the room was done, attention-seeking Kim procrastinated just to keep the cleaning going on and on. Kim prolonged the room-cleaning chores for the attention she received—even negative attention would do—while our more goal-directed Dawn worked hard for the confirmation of her success.

Mom may want her daughters to pick up their room to keep the place looking nice, but why does she have to be right on top of them while they do it? The reason may be that while she thinks having a nice room is the point of the clean-up (a long-term goal), the girls' priorities may be quite short-term—one wants assurances that she is contributing (doing it right); the other wants attention for doing any of it at all!

Mom has *two* strategies to work on. Mom carries out one strategy deliberately, encourage them when they clean their room; the other strategy is an unintentional one of giving unusual attention to Kim's procrastination. So Kim *slows up* for attention, but Dawn *finishes up* for praise.

The solution for Dawn's and Kim's mother came with the insight that Kim needed attention at the end and long after the chore was completed. This attention did not need to be in the form of praise for room-cleaning; it just needed to continue in order to show Kim that finishing the room doesn't finish Mom's attention.

It would be a mistake to conclude that Dawn wants to please Mom and Kim doesn't. Or that Kim just wants to aggravate her mother. These conjectures about sinister Kim would only lead to more nagging and a sour turn in Mom's relationship with Kim. Mom is the adult and *she* had to make the special effort, after room-cleaning, to be interested in Kim.

As a child grows up, blaming the person is increasingly tempting for parents. This can distract parents from looking for chances to give good personal credit when it is deserved. For example, you might know an older child who is moody, disrespectful, rebellious, or cynical. Her parents might think of this as a "long-standing habit" (inside blame): "She has always been that way." But even older children act the way they do partly because of the way they are treated—because of what has ordinarily happened next.

Older children may be disrespectful because the only time they are taken seriously is when they act that way. Their bad behavior may produce an entertaining argument, or their bad talk may seem more "adult" than saying something pleasant. Even some adults believe that!

When the disrespectful child turns happy and cheerful, adults may pat him on the head and tell him he's a "nice boy" but otherwise ignore him. The usefulness of bad behavior in this situation is not lost on the child.

Showing respect for the child by asking for her opinion, showing confidence in her abilities, and doing a good job of listening will bring out an improved form of respect in return. This strategy, an example to be modeled, encourages social behavior that will replace "disrespectful."

Dad: "It's too early to start the garden outside, but we could start

seeds inside. What do you think, Amanda?"
Amanda: What good would that do?"
Dad: "Later, when we plant them outside, they'll have a head start."
Amanda: "Even melons and stuff like that?"
Dad: "Even melons. Let's do melons."

What about Chris? What about Aaron?

When an important complaint has been identified, Mom needs to take it apart and focus on the behaviors that make up the problem. These could be unwanted behaviors that are occurring too much or wanted behaviors that are not happening enough. In Aaron and Chris's family, Chris attracted most of the complaints. When not fighting, the complaint about Chris was that he was not neat. However, while "neat" is a value, it is a vague term and not exactly a behavior. It is a characteristic of many behaviors and not easy to pinpoint when it happens in a six-year-old.

So in this example, before looking for consequences for neatness, we need behaviors that can be easily identified that define neatness. For Chris, we'll need to specify some of these behaviors so we can zero in and provide a clear message to Chris. Then his parents will have a specific signal for their reactions: he combs his hair; he picks up his toys or clothes; he is dressed in clean clothes.

Mom and Dad also complain about Chris's brother, Aaron, for being too aggressive and inconsiderate. His parents will need a different focus that notes when Aaron makes critical and hurtful remarks to others, yells at meals, or hits his brother. Since these are behaviors we don't want, the strategy is going to be tricky, but the definitions about the observable behaviors of Aaron will still make it easier.

> The usefulness of bad behavior is not lost on the child.

Definitions have three goals:
1. To state the specific nature of the problem,
2. To help specify when consequences would be effective, and
3. To guide the search for the most likely *good* behavior to look for first.

This level of behavior must be simple enough and frequent enough to ensure opportunities for support on the *first day* of a new parental rule. And the target behavior must be selected carefully so that Chris and Aaron get enough opportunities for reward to see the rule work.

Setting out a "reasonable demand" for performance is tempting but this may reflect only what the parents think Chris and Aaron *should* be doing. We need a positive rule that takes into account what they are capable of doing now. After things are going well, we can worry about the successive steps necessary to lead them to where they should be.

Mom: "These kids fight too much; it's driving me crazy!"

Dad: "And Chris. He leaves stuff *everywhere*. He's six and it's time he took a little responsibility."

Mom: "This bickering has to end. Are they born this way or is it just that something sets them off?"

Dad: "From now on, if I have to pick up after Chris, whatever I get goes in the closet for an hour before he can have it back."

Mom: "And whenever they fight, I'm going to separate them for half an hour—TV off!"

Mom and Dad have begun to control the situation because they're planning with mutual support; they are being reasonable about punishments; and they're on their way to sorting out the useful parts of blame and credit.

Blame is hard to determine. On the other hand, what's going on can be figured out without fixing blame. And a reasonable plan for a reaction can change what happens next. In many cases the question of who is at fault may not be useful or even important. The useful question is, "What happens next?"

Sorting out how the family members influence each other comes first because the reactions determine the changes in adjustment and habits. Out of all the reasons that influence good behavior and bad, the immediate reactions of parents are the most important.

For example, let's look at all the reasons for the car seat performance of Brian. If Brian is restricted in his car seat, he may be bored, looking for entertainment, and getting the signal that Mom can't do much while driving the car. He fishes around for some action that will produce an entertaining consequence. Now we need to be careful in how we judge consequences and their entertainment value. What seems aversive to us adults may fulfill a purpose in the drab life of our car seat prisoner!

Suppose Brian screams, and Mom scolds him. The scolding has an effect, but not necessarily the one Mom intended. Brian may have felt ignored at the moment, and he may settle for Mom's attention in the scolding. If that's the case, yelling by Brian and scolding by Mom probably make up a regular daily routine.

If Brian wants his sister to be quiet, the scolding may have accomplished that too, even though no scolding was directed at her. Again, a regular routine is likely to develop. Or, the yelling and the scolding may have taken attention away from his sister. He may repeat the routine just for that. For any of these reasons, scolding may support, not reduce, Brian's yelling.

The trading of screams and reprimands and whimpering sisters may be aggravating but the routine may be familiar—and circular: Brian acts up, Mom scolds Brian, sister complains, Mom comforts, Brian gets bored, jealous, or both, and starts another round.

Perhaps this small part of the family connection is set up by Brian's needs—as he sees them—not only for attention but for some challenge from Mom. It is an exchange that at least passes the time from stoplight to stoplight, if an enjoyable alternative is not available.

Brian is too young to be very creative in his solutions, so most Moms would already have thought of bringing along new toys or games kept only in the car. And maybe Brian needs to know that scoldings are not bluffs, and Mom should say, *"Brian, no yelling in the car, that's one!"* If Mom gets to three, she pulls over and stops.

Maybe Mom needs to talk more to Brian in the car about things that interest him—perhaps he needs a little help in practicing conversation, so he won't be so bored:

Brian: "Spiderman! Spiderman!!! Yeaaaaa."
Mom: "Brian, no yelling in the car."
Brian: "Spiderman gets them. Yeah!"
Mom: "Brian, no yelling in the car, that's one. Oh, the trucks are lined up there at the weigh station, more than two!"
Brian: "One, two, three. Three!"
Mom: "Oh! All big ones?"
Brian: "Pretty big."
Mom: "Here's another one, I wonder how heavy he is?"
Brian: "Big."
Mom: "Could Spiderman lift him?"
Brian: "Oh, yes, and push him out of the way!"

Does Mom have to keep up the Spiderman level of conversation all the way home? If Mom were riding with a friend, she would feel obligated to hold up one end of a conversation appropriate for their friendship—it would be a social expectation. So, yes, if Brian is to get practice in acceptable socializing, Mom will need to set an almost continuous example. It's harder for Mom to do with Brian, perhaps, but it is practice for him and he has Mom's effort to imitate. It's not a large part of their family connections but a good habit nevertheless.

Brian's yelling during driving is dangerous and requires a strategy for action. But most behaviors by the Brians of the world don't deserve any planned consequence. While Brian's volume is a problem, *what* Brian talks about in the car may require only the most liberal limits and strategies. Mom can afford to be tolerant and good-natured and talk about Spiderman because it's good practice for Brian and makes for a safer ride.

Routines that lead to self-confidence and self-esteem

A child develops ability to cope when he gains confidence. Practice and experience become crucial ingredients in the development of values and character. For example, learning to use a spoon at dinner comes from using it in the sand box as well as at the dinner table. Learning to use words comes as much from talks in the car as from school vocabulary lessons.

Learning to talk comes from conversations and from listening to the reading of stories and comics where imitation is possible. But in reading to a child, practice may or may not be allowed by the parent. For example, asking the child to tell the story of the Sunday comics after the parent has read them would provide practice in talking *and* in imitating Mom and Dad.

> **Without practice, a child is more dependent on others and her values turn to manipulating others to entertain and care for her.**

Listening itself is not practice. But if the comic strip is simple, the child could practice by telling the story without a preliminary reading by the parent. For more complicated ones, the child can retell them. In this way comics become an entertainment, an enjoyment of talking, telling, and learning. All of this takes time, but what was the point of allowing time for the comics in the first place?

Without practice, a child is more dependent on others and her values turn to manipulating others to entertain and care for her. Life has disadvantages awaiting a girl with little experience deciding when to eat, what to wear, when to wear it, what to say in making a dental appointment, how to entertain herself, and when to conserve money. In childhood and teenage years she will feel a little inadequate, dependent, and may question her own worth. As she leaves the family protection, she will need to learn fast in a situation that is not as loving as the family, and she will bring little confidence to the task.

As a girl or boy who is "untutored" (that is, unpracticed) leaves for college or work or both, their parents will blurt out a last minute barrage of instructions. Whether practice was left out because it seemed to risk too many mistakes, take too much time in the frantic family activities, or was withheld for protection's sake, in the end, parents realize there are consequences to reap. Now they rush to get in all those cautions: "Make sure you brush your teeth, comb your hair, watch out for bad people, start your checking account, and choose friends wisely!"

The first experience of being away from home can be all the more difficult and lonely if our offspring-now-sprung has little confidence in deciding what to wear, when to study, and when to rest.

> **The only place where there is love enough for all that practice is in the family.**

Many of my college students go to a campus counselor with the complaint that no one seems to care about them at the big university. No one wakes them up in the morning, pushes them to do homework, does their laundry. A great deal of the "care" the student misses should have been withdrawn years ago to make room for practice and pride in self. The only place there is love enough for all that practice is in the family.

Most of my students managed to survive the passage from home to campus despite painful evenings learning their size and how to use a washing machine. Lack of practice didn't cause much permanent damage. But in many cases, a critical period of childhood that would have nurtured a knowledge of self-worth, a comfort with life, and fundamental values was missed. Later *complete* development of self-contentment may be difficult or impossible to achieve.

What will make you happy?

Parents start out with a responsibility to make a baby happy and content. We're always evaluating the child's situation and adjusting the diapers, food, and activities to keep the little one happy. It's not surprising that the first source of happiness for a child is his parents, "Mom and

Dad should make me happy."

When you eventually fail in your happiness assignment, your child might get angry, and you might feel guilty or at least your children often try to make you feel that way. We try to teach them to take responsibility for their own happiness but, even as they approach their teenage years, self-sufficiency seems to be an elusive talent in the happiness quest.

For many, a new notion is discovered soon after discovering that parents are not going to be perfect happiness providers. Perhaps things could make me happy, more toys, more plastic, more TV or games, and, not much later, more money. For many, believing that *things* can bring happiness becomes a permanent stage after discovering parental dependency won't do it. All adults feel at times that another house, another car, another job, or more money would do the trick. Maybe it would, but many of us slip back and forth between the "more stuff will do it" theory and a third notion: the "Mr. (or Ms.) Right" happiness theory.

> Happiness is a do-it-yourself project.

Someone out there could be the perfect companion to lean on. Most of us hope to find the special someone, or if we think we have, our confidence in that conclusion varies from day to day. Who is left after Mr. Right comes up short on providing happiness?

After parental dependency until five, a dependency on things until the teens, and a search for the perfect person until you tire of it, happiness turns out to be a do-it-yourself job. We need to look to ourselves, and children need that strength also. Ultimately, children have to shoulder much of the happiness responsibility *themselves*. How will they learn to do that?

First, they will look to you as a model of how time, effort, and perspective contribute to overall feelings of confidence and contentment. Following your lead concerning the value of accomplishments in the creative arts, community, spiritual development, and commitment to an ideal, they will acquire the self-reliance necessary for a fulfilled life. It's another area where your messages need frequent and careful attention.

"Character? The subject never came up!"

When stories about wrong-doing come up in conversation or the media, it's easy to see where the culprit went wrong. Part of the reason the wrongs are more obvious than the rights is that the emphasis is likely to be on the bad news.

But what should have been done? What was the right thing to do? One judge asked a teen accused of mugging, "What did your parents teach you about treating others with respect?" The teen's surprising answer was, "The subject never came up."

Parents don't have to have an answer to questions about character. The main message here is that character questions are important and are OK for discussion. The answers will always be debatable due to circumstances, timing, and the people involved.

> **Questions about character and values are important and OK for discussion.**

Chapter 5
Caution, the Children are Imitating

Imitation is *the* most common human behavior. Not that we don't think for ourselves now and then, but in the huge amount of everyday activities flashed by us, we follow habits and leads from others. The family atmosphere develops from these regular reactions and imitated attitudes. Parental reactions, critical and angry or fair and loving, are copied by the children in their responses back to the parents and on to others. Social habits of children and parents recycle through the family, and everyone reaps a little of what they sow.

Give a Nice Day!

Everyone has seen parents who are always riding their children: "Blow your nose," "Tuck in your shirt," "Don't touch," and so on. On the other hand, we have all seen parents who *never* react and let their children run wild with no consideration for others or their property. Both extremes lead to problems. Where, in the middle ground, is the right style of correction? The frequency of parental reactions may not be as important as the *nature* of all of these little corrections.

Parents who use frequent, but positive, reactions to their children usually have a positive, and less frantic, family situation. A mother who tends to encourage, agree with, and reward or compliment frequently is much more influential and closer to her children than Mom, the critic.

She's just like her mom

Parents try to make their children as *similar* to themselves as possible; they try to instill their standards, their view, their attitude towards community, work, family, religion, and values. It's the way we pass along our culture.

Children and teens try to make themselves as *different* from their parents as possible! They feel a drive to get out from under the umbrella of protection and influence of their parents. That's the way we change and, hopefully, improve our culture!

As your teenager approaches adulthood, positive comments to her, or him, will be your most effective influence.

We stand close and directly in front of our children. What example will we set for the next educators and the next parents? How will we measure up as models and, later, how will our children measure up as parents?

The answer of course is in the time we have for them and the practice they are allowed. Our local paper described a 13-year-old boy's first successful hunting experience with his dad and grandfather; and our adult community education program includes Saturday classes on "Mommy and Me—Crafts," a creative experience in the possibilities of parents and children working together. These are only two small examples of parents getting close to their children where experiences raise not only the child's abilities but also character and respect for themselves. That respect is always good insulation against the temptations of the dangerous teenage behaviors.

All families can develop activities that include everyone. In one family I know, everyone played soccer and encouraged each other's successes on the field. In another, everyone volunteered to ring the bell for the Salvation Army at Christmas. The buzz of conversation about their different experiences with people created common ground as well as valuable social practice. Sports, arts, crafts, community activities—all are excellent training grounds for learning skills, self-respect, and how to get along with others.

How our country, our culture, and our children survive this century depends on how well we do the child-rearing. Possibly our children will only carry our way of life a little further by merely drawing on the last life of the planet, browsing, as other species do, on what the planet has left to offer.

In reacting to everyday problems, children most commonly imitate the adults they are with at home and school, and they imitate style more often than the specific adult behaviors. Attitudes toward others, conversational style, and temperament are the durable characteristics of teachers and parents that are copied. The result is a general disposition made up of habits and styles of encouragement or punishment of others. A child can easily acquire a disposition almost entirely from the family air!

The disposition to punish and correct others can be learned just as easily as the disposition to encourage others but the results are vastly different. Punishment shows that out of all the responses the child could have made, he has chosen the wrong one—try again. Little information is available in that.

A positive reaction is much more efficient because it says that of all the things he could have done, this is one of the right ones. A rewarding reaction is more difficult for parents to come up with because it takes time to decide what to reward and how to do it. We're more likely to already know what we want to punish and how we would do it. But with a positive approach you have a more pleasant job as a parent and you have a child who is still informative, friendly, responsive, and not always wanting to go somewhere else!

> **With a positive approach, you have a more pleasant job as a parent and your child will not always want to go somewhere else.**

The choice between rewards and punishments will be taken up in detail in Chapter 6, but in most cases the odds favor the positive approach.

Learning to police your disposition is a difficult task. No one is planning consequences for *you* as an adult, and adults change by practice with encouragements just as children do. So whether or not anything can be done about the dispositions in your home depends on the answer to the question, "Can you control yourself through conscientious effort and through feedback from your partner?"

If you are a single parent, it may be all the more difficult to say to yourself, as a spouse might: "Don't let me pick on the kids; stop me and point out my good reactions."

The disposition of the family can also be influenced by planning for the small everyday social behaviors of kids. Many parents have developed a poor disposition in their child by not planning the limits of *their own demands* as carefully as they plan the limits on the kids. For example, in what situations will the child be on his own? A child makes so many mistakes. Without planning, parents feel that they have to be after the kids constantly and one parent may complain to the other, "Why can't you just leave her alone?"

The answer is that, without a plan, Mom or Dad cannot be sure what "right" should be encouraged and what "wrong" should be discouraged. They can't leave the child alone because they always find the problems.

"Isn't it amazing how mother and daughter are alike!" said Ms. Jones. "That woman reading at the end of the back row just *has* to be Regina's mother. Regina even reads at lunch time!"

"Yes, it's unbelievable," whispered Ms. Miller. "I'd recognize Bobby Comic's father anywhere with little jokes. And Lisa Sour's father sulking while he waits for the meeting, you wouldn't believe such details could be inherited!"

Ms. Jones and Ms. Miller were teachers at PTA back-to-school night. They told me that when they were waiting for the meeting to start, they played a "Match the New Parents Game." It's been their favorite for years, and they find their guesses to be very accurate. Their success with matching parents and students comes, in part, from physical similarities that are inherited, but they find another hint in the way the students act which is often a close copy of their parents' style. How talkative, pleasant, sarcastic, or happy each parent and student seems to be, helps the teachers make their matches, and they are very successful.

When children imitate bad dispositions, they must use threats in a subtle way, of course, because they are less powerful than adults. Fighting back, a child puts off his parents or teacher and may reduce their requests for work. A child creates more parental reactions in return, and he sees that as confirmation of his cynical expectations of others.

Consider Lisa, eight years old. She has developed a negative attitude so in school she is cynical and pessimistic. You can imagine that it's easy to feel uncomfortable or aggravated around her. At home with her family, Lisa receives a bit more attention, but the aggravation and frustration that others feel usually shows through:

Mom: "How was school today, Lisa?"
Lisa: "OK."
Mom: "Well, tell me about it!"
Lisa: "Do you have to know everything?"
Mom: "I was just interested."
Lisa: "Just leave me alone."

Lisa is a non-rewarder, thinking little of others, and asking little from them. She's no trouble, but somehow she's still troublesome. She brings out the worst in others and then reacts to the responses she draws by getting worse herself. The cycle continues. To break the cycle, someone will have to be big enough to not play the game. That requires love, because it means performing good social behavior with no support from Lisa, possibly with punishment, mild as it may be, from her instead.

Lisa herself might grow up enough to be the "someone" who will break the cycle someday. However, in the short run, it's not likely that anyone will spontaneously change. The most likely adjustment Lisa will make is to "give them back what they give you." If they give you bad behavior, let them taste their own medicine! Punishment for punishment; silence for silence, or even, silence for punishment (they won't get anything out of me!).

Lisa may extend her use of punishment and later learn to use warnings of punishments to coerce teacher or parent. If demands are not met, she increases the intensity of the demand, and then she tries further punishment—possibly a tantrum. It's coercion. Adults may learn to avoid all this punishment by giving in early.

Giving in serves as reward to Lisa, but it also rewards the adults because they successfully avoid Lisa's escalating tantrum.

This is a common parent-child relationship. *The child's bad behavior is rewarded* by getting undeserved privileges and avoiding work, and *the parent's "giving in" is rewarded* by successfully avoiding the threat of more bad behavior.

In order to have an effect on Lisa, adults need to model a positive disposition for her. It's a big order because that is not what comes to mind when you are around Lisa and the change is not going to be quick.

Tough times produce some weird behavior.
Parents are often amazed at the variety of behaviors—both good and bad—their children show. If you find it difficult to sort out what good behaviors you want, then you can see how difficult it will be for them to find out how they should behave. Of all the possibilities, what will they try first in a new situation? Most of the time they will try what worked best for them last time or in a similar situation. If nothing comes to mind, they may try out what you do! If it works for you, maybe it will work for them.

A checklist for keeping an eye on your model disposition:
1. How many positive remarks do I make to my kids each day?
2. Am I modeling good social skills and tolerance?
3. Do my rules create an atmosphere *I* enjoy?
4. How many rules can I have and still maintain a pleasant atmosphere?

5. Could I reduce the rules that require policing and enforcement?

The checklist can be a handy helper. For example, a father and mother came to me for help in dealing with their son whose main difficulty was his disrespect for others, particularly his mother. "Disrespect" was defined as making sarcastic remarks, ignoring direct questions, and insulting people. Dad said he thought Mom contributed to the problem by being "wishy-washy" and not "standing up to him, even if she is a woman." He thought she probably got this attitude from spending time in "big conferences" with some of her "silly friends." No doubt Dad's disrespect was obvious to his son and provided a terrible example.

It was easy to see where we needed to start. However, the father was surprised that it was with the example he set for his son. The habit had become strong and his son expected praise and admiration for his abusive behavior from his father. As we will see in Chapter 7, cooperation and support between parents is needed for extra consistency and it becomes an example to children of how to treat their parents!

> Dad's disrespect was obvious to his son and provided a terrible example.

Six-year-old Taylor is another example of a parent model gone bad. Taylor came into our office waiting room first and sat on a convenient chair. The mother chose to sit at the opposite side of the seating area. "Sit over here," she said. He moved to the seat next to her. "Don't swing your foot like that!" Taylor picked up a magazine from the table. "Be careful with that," she said. He turned a page noisily. "Shh, I *told* you to be careful!"

As it turned out, one of the complaints from Mom and Taylor's teachers was that *Taylor* was bossy and constantly critical of others! Mom had developed an attitude of criticism, low expectations, and low tolerance, and it was contagious. Picking up on the cue, Taylor developed his own habit of being critical of others.

Learned dispositions

An interesting aspect of a parental disposition such as the one displayed by Taylor's mother is that generally a parent uses it only with the child. Tiger Moms, a later subject in this chapter, do not ordinarily act in this punitive way with adults. Rather, they seem to have high expectations for their children and present a model of those expectations to their children. But often the expectations themselves have never been thoughtfully worked out. What at first appears to be a high standard of behavior by Taylor's mother turns out to be actually *no specific* standard at all. So a parent in such a situation punishes nearly everything and finds no opportunity to reward good behavior.

One teacher I talked to was surprised that Taylor was having problems, "I know he can be difficult, but I have decided to catch him doing well. I focus on finding his good moments and when I find one, I let him know it. I think he knows I'm giving him a chance and that I like him."

Adults expect the same of us. More tolerance and chances to make amends for mistakes, and we show them a better disposition. What is expected of us and what we expect create the social atmosphere we live in. The adult rule is, "Don't correct or reprimand until a mistake has been made. Certainly withhold punishment, it creates bad feelings." Here's one reason the social climate is better in the teachers' coffee room than in the hallway.

Another teacher I know said that when she went down the school hallway, she noticed students reacting to their teachers in ways that were "typical" of each teacher's classes. She was surprised that the students could make such quick adjustments as they went from Math to Art to Gym, creating a recognizable atmosphere in each place.

> **What is expected of us and what we expect creates the social atmosphere we live in.**

From a selfish point of view, if you were a teacher how would you like to spend your day? With people who are modeling adult positive attitudes or people who are modeling a punishing disposition?

When this praise is consistently used in an obvious manner for a particular behavior, results are usually good, and an additional improvement comes when the attitude is imitated. Some parents and teachers may devalue the effect of their attention because they observe only an immediate target behavior. In the longer view, however, a child's disposition will become a close copy of the surrounding adult attitudes.

Give a nice day.

The problem illustrated by Taylor's mother while she was waiting for counseling is often the result of a lack of planning and attention to parental reactions. The critical part of planning that is left out is determining which behaviors are important and which are trivial. Had Mom ever thought about whether Taylor should always sit next to her?

She said she had not. Why had she corrected him to do so? She said she was afraid he "might do something wrong over there." She said she had no specific fear he would do anything wrong, she just didn't trust him. Some boys might deserve such distrust, but for Taylor it was just habit with a little reprimand thrown in. A psychological leash had been put on, and it was jerked regularly.

To break the habit of the psychological leash, a good rule is, "Don't correct or instruct your child until you are certain a mistake is being made." This is the rule that all adults expect you to apply to them, and your children deserve the same treatment until they prove otherwise. Mom and Dad should train themselves to hesitate before reprimanding, correcting or discouraging a behavior that is not worth the bad feeling.

When Taylor's mom tried the "catch 'em being good" suggestion, she told Taylor how well he was doing on a part of his homework and, another time, how well he had cleaned up his room. He said, "Didn't know you cared." Not a very encouraging response, but if Taylor's mom keeps up the positive, the psychological leash can be broken.

The psychological leash is worth breaking for additional reasons. Corrections intended as reprimands may become rewards over a long time. They also replace the child's responsibility. He just does what he wants while he depends on his parents to make all the corrections. So while striving for perfection, total dependence is achieved.

And, to keep it all going, the corrections may come to function as rewards because they are attention. In addition, a disposition is still being learned, of course, and *the child* may learn the habit of nagging as well. She may bring up certain questions continually and may harp on them often:

Cassie: "But Mommy, why *can't* I walk to the movies alone?"
Mom: "I already told you why, Cassie."
Cassie: "I know, but can't I, pleeease!"
Mom: "No."

The next day it starts all over again:

Cassie: "Mommy, Mary wants me to walk to the movies with her. Can I go?"

What events maintain Cassie's nagging? The topic always brings disagreement and punishment, but she continues to bring it up. The first and most likely reason for this running battle is that Mom and Dad have never held a brief planning session about the problem. Without this strategy session, the reasons given to Cassie change from time to time; her parents disagree from time to time; and they lose confidence in these decisions. The inconsistency encourages Cassie to keep trying because one day she thinks she might hit the right combination of attitudes and get to go. She probably will.

The planning session would nail down the reasons, pinpoint the agreement between Cassie's parents and give them confidence. It would help by stating the honest reasons for the decisions in detail.

Mom: "Your father and I have decided you can't walk to the movies alone. We think bigger people might make trouble for you along the way and while you're there. When you are 12 you may do it. Right, David?"

Dad: "Right."

Now will Cassie stop nagging? Probably not, but the amount of nagging will decrease, and Cassie will be happier because the situation is now clear and fair—at least Cassie's parents think so and it gives them confidence. For Cassie, the structure makes the situation more comfortable than the continual argument, although it's still not what she wants. Cassie's argumentative behavior will mellow because the statement of the rule is concrete and detailed—not much room for loopholes.

> **A good disposition begins by imitating yours.**

As the air clears, Cassie's parents need to stay alert and make a special effort to engage and encourage her. They don't want this vacuum to fill with some other unwanted attention-getting behavior. A good disposition begins with imitation, and it is maintained by experience with reliable rules that produce opportunities to support good social and emotional habits.

Looking only for mistakes is not good for either the parent's or the child's morale. It reduces the overall amount of behavior which reduces risk-taking by the child and, therefore, learning.

In this way, two general characteristics of love and a good relationship are violated: the child is not given the benefit of the doubt and the child's growth is kept in check by the threat. It is often the *good behavior* that is reduced by frequent punishment—even mild punishment. Chapter 6 will present alternatives.

Punishment includes reprimands, scoldings, and sarcastic comments designed to reduce bad behavior in children along with many "left-handed" compliments—punishments disguised as rewards: "That's certainly a big improvement over yesterday!" or "That's very good, considering..."

These statements with double meanings should be watched carefully. Children are less capable of sorting out the subtle meanings and are likely to get only the literal message that they are *still wrong*.

When a child is right, send a clear, positive message without complicated verbal decorations.

Parents need time for planning these child-rearing strategies. This may sound devious and scheming. But remember how much time and energy your children use for working things out their way, even though they may not be aware of their own intentions as they react, adjust, and react again. With the advantage of time available for planning and trying out solutions over and over, children can gain too much control over the family activity. Occasional planning sessions can keep the balance and fairness in family relationships.

What is good behavior and where can I get some?

In order to know when to react, a clear description of the behavior is necessary so that you'll identify it when you see it. If you make a bet concerning which of two children will be first to share a toy with a new child, how will you decide who wins the bet? A precise definition of "sharing" is needed. It's not like betting on a horse race where everyone knows what a "winner" is—especially now that we have photographs of the finish. A bet on a child's sharing can be a much more difficult problem in definitions.

We need an objective definition of "sharing" and then agreement on what to look for. Otherwise, there's too much room for interpretation, and the bettors will always argue. For example, if a child offers one of his toys to another child, that will be called sharing for the purposes of the bet. It is not necessary to know *why* the child shares or what is on the child's mind at the moment.

He may share because the adult wagers are watching, or he may share to get a toy from the other child, or for other "wrong" reasons. But a bet's a bet, and if the parents want to support sharing in their child, they will need a similar definition, and they too will not know the child's mind at any moment.

Definitions help parents agree on when encouragement—concrete payoff or social praise—will be given. This decision is important. If parents agree on what the good behavior is, then it becomes the signal for parental attention.

In addition to making things clear, well-defined rules about what is right also give the child the advantage of quickly understanding what *to do*. If frequent little talks and explanations seem necessary, the definition itself, or the reaction to it, may be too vague or variable. The goal here is consistent, repeated practice with a reasonable, and very obvious, consequence.

For the purpose of the bet, the behavioral definition of sharing was one child offering a toy to another. When the child drifts away from sharing, by, say, snatching a toy from his playmates, the temptation to correct or reprimand such a "mistake" deserves careful consideration. A reprimand or correction, is a new behavior in the situation. It runs the risk of being more effective as attention than as the negative it was intended to be.

The bet, as originally stated, is about sharing. Mistakes, such as snatching a toy from others, is a different behavior and not part of the bet. In most cases ignoring the mistakes and emphasizing the positive is best. In Chapter 6, we will take up alternatives to punishment as reactions to errors and mistakes.

How much explanation is required for children?

Not all the whys and wherefores concerning a request from a child need prolonged explanations. Explanations are important when a new rule is to go into effect, but repeated requests for explanations may be just a form of filibustering to get the rule changed or to postpone it. What is important for learning and for reliable and desirable behavior patterns is a consistent relationship between action and parental *re*action.

When you learn to drive a car, you don't understand all the complicated mechanisms of the car. An understanding of pistons, cams, and ignition systems is not necessary. As long as the accelerator, brake, steering wheel, and ignition key work consistently, you can learn very well. Learning becomes a nightmare if the car is difficult to start, has inconsistent brakes, or sloppy steering.

> **Repeated explanations may become attention instead.**

In the same way, a child can gain experience from a reliable set of rules and policies without knowing all the adult reasoning behind the rules. Consistency is enough; understanding how the car engine works or why parents are anxious about certain situations may help, but it is not required.

Detailed courses on internal combustion engines would be a waste of time for driving schools. At some stages, it may be a waste of time to continually tell a child about germs when asking him to wash his hands before eating. An occasional reminder might be useful even at age three, but repeated explanations may become attention for dirty hands.

A study concerning this issue was conducted by E. R. Guthrie and G. P. Horton in the early years of psychology. In their experiments, a cat was placed in a problem box. As most cat owners know, cats enjoy exploring small spaces, but it is not in a cat's nature to be content in a confined place. A pole in the center of the box could open the door if the cat pushed it, but because the cat didn't know about the pole, it tried various actions to escape. It mewed and scratched at first, and then as it paced around, it accidentally bumped the pole and gained its freedom. This was not an insight any more than a child's first use of a doorknob is an insight. It was an accident. Nevertheless, a certain behavior did produce a good result, and when the cat was again put in the box, it was a little faster getting out.

History does not tell us how many scratches Guthrie and Horton suffered, but they did put the cat into the box several times. The cat escaped faster and faster by rubbing the pole in the way a cat rubs a person's leg, thus releasing the latch. The cat didn't have to learn about latches and springs and hinges. Mechanical engineering is above the mind of a cat. It didn't face the pole, grab it, or scratch it. It only learned the necessary: stand here, swing your rear so you rub the pole, leave.

Most of the everyday behaviors learned by children are also learned without a complete understanding of the processes involved. From rattles and noisy toys, to spoons, doorknobs, computers, and TV remotes, to pleasing Daddy and Mommy, their skills develop and race far ahead of their understanding. Children, and adults at times, only understand that certain activities produce good results and often that's enough. So it's best to be brief and conservative with explanations of rules—especially when a son or daughter seems to be enjoying the argument.

The advantage enjoyed by Guthrie and Horton's cat was that it was placed in a situation where success was likely. The box was not room size and the pole was not broom size. The rule was about a behavior well within the cat's ability.

The set up was good, and the planned consequence, the escape, was ready and delivered quickly. As a learning strategy, it had all the right ingredients. The process of specifying how a behavior will result in a planned consequence is the strategy.

The word "strategy," when applied to child-rearing, may at first imply a little too much struggling, a little too much confrontation, or even scheming. And there is a little of each of these in adult-rearing. The important thing is to devote time and effort to conscious, routine planning. Think about how much time and energy children have for figuring out how to accomplish their goals! Parents who neglect planning enter every child-rearing situation one step behind their children.

When I ask parents in training groups to spend 15 to 30 minutes each week in a strategy session, most parents find it difficult to set aside that time. On the other hand, their children, with no jobs and few domestic responsibilities, have plenty of time for planning tryouts of new ideas and methods on their parents. It is a blessing that children are poor time managers!

Children are not all scheming little devils, but they do constantly test and experience their family situations, like the cat, only with more thought. If parents of a 15-year-old have lost some control over their son or daughter, it might be due to the many hours of the last few years the teenager spent searching for solutions to frustrations compared with the number of hours his or her parents spent thinking through plans for change.

So the planning session is a necessity. It allows parents to regroup, to compromise in private, and to agree on a united front. It ensures that the behavior of concern will be recognized and consequences will be consistent. It need not be secretive. In most cases, telling your son or daughter the results of the session is beneficial. If a strategy will only work if the children don't know what it is, then it's unlikely to work, is a little dishonest, and it's probably unrealistic because the children will find out.

In the single parent situation, the compromises, the agreement, and the united front may have to take place in one's own mind, but that may be the most important place for consistency anyway.

Tiger Mom's model

In *Battle Hymn of the Tiger Mother*, Tiger Mom (Amy Chua) put aside her interest in her two daughters and replaced it with days filled with music practice and homework hours designed to see that the children avoided the disgrace of getting a "B" in school. Success was all that counted.

What did the children think of that? We don't know because Mom never asked and probably didn't care. When the children balked at doing their daily hours of violin and piano practice before completing hours of homework perfectly, she browbeat them with threats, "You can't stay in the house if you don't listen to Mommy."

Chua's "Battle hymn" is a no-nonsense approach to child-rearing that leaves no doubt who is in charge and who is setting the goals and the daily agenda for each child. A's in school and first place in violin and piano are the only acceptable grades or outcomes. Mommy knows best and the little person's interests or thoughts on the matter are not important and shouldn't be part of the selected activities which are to be practiced until perfect.

The essence of tough Chinese parenting, according to Chua, is this demand for all-out effort in childhood endeavors. She is not native Chinese. She grew up in the American Midwest, so she might not be correct in her description of what goes on over there.

Tiger Mom wants prodigies no matter how the children suffer. "Bully Mom" would be a better description.

If Chua were training high jumpers in track she might focus her effort on a few with great potential. She would see that some of us are just too small or have legs too short. Even with great pressure from Chua, we will not be "successful" by Chua's standards. In her daughter's cases, we don't know if they have "legs too short" or just need more pressure from their coach who has the confidence of a parent but not the common sense.

> **Tiger Mom wants prodigies no matter how the children suffer. "Bully Mom" would be a better description.**

Another disadvantage of the Tiger-Mom approach is that the child's view is entirely discounted as if the child has no idea of what talents he has or which activities deserve extended practice. What if Chua's daughters had talents in other areas not of interest to Mom?

This happened when one daughter finally quit violin lessons, Mom was very unhappy. She had no idea if her daughter was gifted in music let alone the violin specifically. If her daughter was interested in playing guitar would things have worked out better? I doubt Mom ever asked because there are few trophies or concerts for guitars. Tiger-Mom thought she would have no chance to be proud.

Chua does offer some useful observation. For example, she says western parents often give heaps of praise when a child's accomplishment is close to nothing, This habit reduces self-esteem because real accomplishment is viewed as no better than a casual attempt.

With nothing to strive for, the child may have no reason to try harder. Some of us locals could learn from Chua's suggestion of holding off on undeserved praise. But Chua would hold off on almost all praise because she's never quite satisfied.

If Mom's routine reaction to her child's interests is negative, and she has no respect for anything outside of the preferences of her adult friends, she may say, "Put that guitar out of your mind and get to work." If her daughter fails to impress others after hard work, her daughter may not try again. Instead she may wander into bad habits and become a victim of the fanatics that troll the troubled waters of the teenage years.

The best parental strategy will include supporting the desirable, ignoring the tolerable, and reacting with logical, mild, and consistent reprimands to the intolerable. This plan will give children a good model to follow as well as a way to learn. They will become more competent and pleasant people. Even Tiger Mom may come to like them!

Trophy children

Loving parents of gifted children just want their special sons and daughters to use their talents and be happy doing it.

These remarkable children are a challenge. At age three the challenge is great fun—they want to learn so much. At age 10, they are changing fast and the challenge is more serious—they demand so much. At age 15, the challenge can be a real chore—they want to *control* so much!

Precocious children blossom early and develop rapidly probably because of so much "adult" experience—second hand—from TV, music, videos, Internet, talk shows, movies, radio, and peers with similar information and misinformation. Some expansion of their minds and insight seems good, but too much of it can be disturbing.

Irregular profiles.

Some unusual abilities that challenge parents, math and language skills, for example, also attract the respect and focus of school programs. Others, social skills and common sense, for example, are not as carefully evaluated or valued by school programs. Yet unrecognized talents can still contribute to the success and happiness of parents and of a child growing up. So I would advocate a broad view of "gifted and talented." All children have unusual abilities and most abilities deserve some nurturing.

The first time most parents realize their children are thinking beyond their years is when they first encounter unusual questions:

"Why don't you and Dad have more children? You have more eggs, don't you?"

"Why doesn't the president just kill all the bad people?"

"Can I try some beer?"

"What are sexual hair bents? Isn't it just a difference in haircuts?"

(She meant "sexual harassment!")

"Why doesn't Aunt Andrea make Uncle Bill just go away?"

"Why is the moon just the right size to cover the sun?"

"Will the cat go to heaven?"

Not all of these remarks may strike you as indicating genius, but they do indicate that an intellect is beginning to stir, and his questions are about more than immediate concerns.

My local school wants to test the children to find out how many gifted and talented children they have. Why do they want to know? How do you determine what test and what scores indicate gifted or talented?

So why do we ask? Because we value some talents over others and provide special attention only for students strong in the areas we test. Yet strengths that lead to success are not the same as those in our definition of gifted, nor is success easily defined in the first place!

> **Social skills and common sense are not as carefully evaluated or valued by school programs.**

The nagging reason may be that we test for the "gifted" because we want "trophy children." In order to have trophy children you have to have a contest.

Don't be misled by society's narrow views of gifts and talent. Look and keep looking, all through their growing-up years, for your own child's gifts.

Some parents of gifted children have told me they are often aggravated by their talented child's failure to follow through on projects. Why do children frequently start projects that later falter? Why would a daughter procrastinate on practicing her music when she was so excited at first? Why would she keep missing practice by letting the hours go by? You could be content with a less than perfect student rather than risk giving attention to the procrastination. Or, it may be time to increase support for smaller steps.

Procrastination may be only the fear of not being perfect! We need to be careful that our standards don't discourage effort. If your son "takes in" a standard from his parent that is too high, he may never get started for fear of coming up short of the mark. You never know until you try, but also, you won't fail if you don't try!

If the goal of music lessons is enjoyment of music then the little steps along the way are the ones to encourage, the pursuit of perfection was never the purpose. Has her understanding of music increased? It's hard to know. One can only support the activity and set a good example through interest. Since progress toward a television debut is not the point, why not just join in her interest and forget perfection?

> **Look and keep looking for your own child's gifts.**

Overlooking a child's grumpy reaction to a project is a challenge for parents, but more may be happening than is apparent to either parent or child:

Alisha: "These art museums are boring."
Mom: "Some of these paintings are very famous and beautiful."
Alisha: "They're all *old* pictures of *old* people."
Mom: "But look at this one. Can you see how the artist used light and dark to show how the light comes from the candle?"
Alisha: "I could do that."
Mom: "And look at this one. Look at how some things are made to look far away."
Alisha: "They're just smaller."
Mom: "But they are just the right sizes, and a little less clear."
Alisha: "I guess."

Is grumpy Alisha getting a new appreciation of art? Perhaps not, but don't conclude that Alisha's museum trip is a waste of time just because of her attitude. Remember, sometimes children feel an *obligation* to make you believe you are not having an effect! Later on, when she encounters other art or tries out her own painting skills again, you may get a better indication of the usefulness of the museum trip. Keep your own spirits up on the museum trip and guard against following your child into a gloomy attitude. More may be getting done than it seems.

Regardless of your approach to museum trips or child-rearing in general, the question of whether anything has changed in the mind of the child will remain partially unanswered. All parental efforts will seem only partly successful. The children, needing proof they are persons in their own right, want it that way.

Chapter 6
Discipline: You can't make a garden by just pulling weeds

If "get tough" means making the hard decisions and sticking to them, I'm all for it. If it means explaining why the enforcement of hard rules and limitations are really in the best interest of the child, I'm sure we're all in support of that. But if you take "get tough" to mean more frequent and more severe punishment for children while they are small enough, it's wrong for many reasons.

First of all, it's wrong when they are young and innocent. Before age two, we call it abuse. After 18 we might call the police. In between, when they get big enough, the kids will learn how to avoid it, or hit back, or run for it. You can't make a garden just by pulling weeds. A child punished frequently will begin searching for someone who looks for more than weeds.

There's not much information in, "Wrong!" A young person looking for the right thing to do needs instruction and support more than punishment for mistakes.

Of course, parents must use their control over the children to limit them and prevent as much of the dangerous behavior as possible. Reprimands, limits, pointing out the mistakes and the five alternatives to punishment coming later in this chapter—all are necessary to help a child learn while parents retain some control.

Physical punishment is especially dangerous because the effects are widespread and, as frustration sets in, parents may feel the only way out is to increase the force.

The debate about punishment is reserved for children, of course. When they become adults, or just get too big, we all try to find something else. How you discipline your children will set a standard that they will carry on and use in their own families. What example do you want to give them?

Uncle Harry's hard line won't help

"You're too easy on Jessica and Juan! Let me have them for a week, they'll shape up after a couple of swats from their Uncle Harry!"

Jessica and Juan, seven and eight years old, can be real trouble as a sister and brother team in a game of "Let's-push-them-to-the-edge." They act up or throw tantrums for attention, or they tease and fight with each other just for entertainment and attention.

Any suggestion to Jessica or Juan by their parents that they do "something nice" is rejected, perhaps because that would mean the game would be over.

"Get Tough" relatives like Uncle Harry assume that stern talk and a few extra swats would fix the Jessica-and-Juan problem. Uncle Harry thinks he would somehow use punishment more effectively and more consistently. He's on the wrong track for several reasons.

Why Uncle Harry is wrong

Reason No. 1: Uncle Harry's hard-line approach will be, must be, inconsistent.

The first problem with Uncle Harry's use of punishment is that even Uncle Harry cannot, *and should not*, be consistent. Straight punishment would be too inhuman without the inconsistencies of warnings and threats.

> **When a child is right, send a clear, positive message of approval.**

If Uncle Harry's swats were as consistent and as quick as, say, a shock from an electric outlet, he might make some short-term progress. Misused wall outlets and lamp sockets consistently punish you without warning; they don't give you a break because you look cute and "devilish." And you don't get a break because you've had a bad day or haven't been reminded lately of what will happen if you touch the wrong part. We get none of this consideration, and we all take the necessary precautions.

But Uncle Harry is not a wall socket. Out of love and sympathy, neither Mom, Dad, nor Uncle Harry can resist preceding punishments with the deserved warnings and threats that become part of the game.

Parental consistency is always desirable and basic to learning. The lack of consistent reactions when using rewards leads to confusion and slows the progress. Little inconsistent rewards are not avoidable and don't do much harm. Large amounts of inconsistent punishment bring on many problems and the effect is damaging.

Remember that "mean" teacher you had in school? He, or maybe it was a she, used punishments, reprimands, sarcastic remarks, put-downs, and embarrassments whenever the kids deviated from the desirable, and sometimes even when her students had done nothing wrong. I bet you hated that class!

A student's greatest fear is to be embarrassed in front of the class. With "Miss Meany," you just couldn't be sure when you might trigger an embarrassing reaction. *All* behaviors (even volunteering right answers, suggestions, or questions) were reduced because you and your friends just wouldn't risk it. Not surprisingly, most "mean" teachers think the children in their classes are not very smart.

When punishment is uncertain, children become cautious, especially when they are around the punisher. But around other people, a child's bad behavior may increase to let off the oppressed steam or to somehow even the score.

Parents can also fall into the "mean teacher" pattern, and their children may learn to behave whenever Mom threatens or looks mad. As Mom realizes this works, she may take up "looking (and acting) mad" most of the time. She may soon find that "looking mad" won't do, and she may have to act "really mad." Now Mom has been pushed up a notch toward becoming a behavior problem herself!

> **Victims of unpredictable punishment find that they can better predict punishment by watching their parents' emotions than by respecting agreements and requests.**

So for Jessica and Juan to grow into happy, independent, productive adults, they need opportunities to do more interesting activities than their "Let's-push-them-to-the-edge game." Mom and Dad need to catch opportunities to encourage their kids, limiting the use of punishment with better alternatives. Uncle Harry needs to learn about allowing the kids to make amends for mistakes as we adults do. More on alternatives later.

Carrying out all of this is much more difficult and requires a lot more planning than hard-headed Uncle Harry's idea of "thrashing it out of them."

Reason No. 2: The terror of the parent trigger.

Uncle Harry's inconsistency is based in part on his own level of frustration and may not be entirely predictable by a child. When he's finally had it *up to here*, it triggers his explosion. If you are too young to tell Uncle Harry's moods, these ugly surprises can become terrorizing when you miss the cues.

Experiments in psychology show that just a few unforgettable, unexpected punishments can stop learning and cancel taking any risks of making mistakes for a long time. All creativity stops.

So when parental punishment is likely to be more related to the frustrations and moods of the parent than to the mistakes of the child, terror, or at least intimidation, sets in. These terrorized children are more interested in the moment-to-moment mood of their parents than in their own rights and wrongs.

Once children of "unpredictable" punishment have figured out it is Mom (or Dad) they need to watch, they learn how to use the discovery. They will watch, drive their parents down the road to misery, and pull up just short of the boiling points of Mom and Dad.

In this situation, children become manipulators who know that as long as they don't push too far, they're safe. They find that they can better predict punishment by watching their parents' emotions than by respecting agreements and requests. The parent-child relationship will suffer because the practice of "punish-when-I've-had-it" tempts children to react to parents with disrespect, silence, and deceit, and to avoid them altogether when they can.

Reason No. 3: Children will imitate.

We usually think of a child's imitation of parents as very specific. "Look at the way he walks, just like his dad." "Look at the way she does her hair, trying to be just like Mom!"

But as mentioned earlier, copying Mom and Dad is more likely to involve social habits. How does Mom handle situations when things don't go right? What is her solution when others don't do what she wants? If Dad gets frustrated, how does he react?

We all know how quickly kids pick up those words of frustration when Dad hits himself on the kitchen drawer, but they also pick up the cues on *how to react* when requests are ignored. Kids can get the message that punishment is a good way (used by Mom and Dad) to deal with people.

The imitation of punishment will include the child's social life. How should a child handle friends when they don't do the "right thing?" "It works for Mom; maybe it will work for me." In any case, the most natural reflex to punishment is to give some back. If it is not possible to punish the parent, the child will turn to others.

Children make a lot of mistakes: being led into errors by peers, forgetting chores and commitments, indulging in unhealthy foods, and wasting time, to mention a few. When parents see so many errors it's difficult to be accepting and look to the long run. But the goal of teaching how to react to others by imitation may be more important than correcting the mistake itself.

Reason No. 4: Punishment is insulting, belittling, and lowers a child's value of himself.

The emotional put-down of punishment distracts the child from learning about the desired behavior. The punishment act, itself, is childish and belittles the significance and power of the person who is punished. That's why *adults* are so insulted if you try punishment on them!

Many parents have seen this downturn in a child's value of himself as he progresses through school. If a teacher's criticism is too severe, the child's self-esteem starts down, the fear starts up, and a new disadvantage to learning develops. The fear of failure begins to reduce the childhood process of trial and error.

The discoveries in school subjects, and in learning to get along with others, come from a lot of guesses. How much guessing will a frightened child do? Once a child is discouraged and engaged in self-degrading thoughts, parents and teachers know learning will be slow.

> **Once a child is discouraged and engaged in self-degrading thoughts, learning will be slow.**

Here's an example of this broader negative effect of punishment from the animal world. For many years I taught a college course in animal learning. Students had to teach a pigeon to perform tasks by rewarding small successes. The first task was to get the pigeon to peck a plastic disc by first rewarding it with seeds for stepping toward the disc, then putting its head toward it, then touching it, and finally pecking the disc.

Sometimes students had trouble with the project because their pigeon was too scared to even move in its cage. If it had been handled roughly or temporarily escaped and had to be chased down before being put in the learning cage, it was too upset to do anything. Pigeons that won't *do anything* can't be taught *anything*!

Often, it was a stand off. The student stared at the pigeon waiting for a chance to reward success. The pigeon stared at the student waiting for a chance to get out! The solution was usually a new effort in careful handling and generous rewards for even the smallest movements to explore the cage, followed by rewards for exploring the plastic disc, etc.

Punishment can produce the same impasse between child and parent. The solution, in principle, is similar as well: careful handling and generous support.

Reason No. 5: Punishment encourages stress behaviors.

Punishment will encourage bad habits such as nail-biting, hair-twirling, and obsessions with video games and TV. These routines are very stubborn habits maintained by their usefulness in avoiding contact with the punisher.

Whenever encouragement and reward are unlikely, these stress behaviors will increase. Stress behaviors can attract parental attention, and we are on our way to a new long-term problem!

Reason No. 6: The power struggle.

Punishment will tempt a child to react to the parent with disrespect; this takes over the family airways leaving little time for positive interactions and learning. The parent may be the more powerful, but the child will still try to give a good showing in the struggle.

The power struggle of punishment can spread to all family members as the children delight in finding Mom's or Dad's mistakes and "punish" as best they dare. As others pick up the habit, a competition develops. Who can "outdo" (put down, criticize, reprimand, catch more mistakes of) whom? It ruins the family as a nurturing place where learning is encouraged through practice and mistakes are tolerated.

Reason No. 7: It's a short-term improvement trap.

The parental bad habit of using punishment can be stubborn because it produces short-term results. For example, Erin has aggravated his Aunt Hazel all day and now refuses to get in the car to go home. Harried Hazel grabs Erin, gives him a little extra squeeze, and roughly deposits him in his seat belt. Then, for the moment, we have progress—Erin is closer to home! Erin's bad behavior is temporarily stopped, Hazel has released a little tension, and maybe "taught Erin a lesson" or at least, evened the score.

The long-term disadvantages of Hazel's punishment habit will grow slowly. Erin will start bad escape habits, he will feel worse about himself and about Aunt Hazel, and he will try to use punishment himself to "get even." These two people are well on the way to a poor relationship where Erin tries to get back at Aunt Hazel and watches for her boiling point, and Aunt Hazel boils over now and then to gain temporary relief from Erin's bad moments. Erin will learn when to let up a little, and he may also learn to imitate her punishment to gain more control.

Reason No. 8: Discrimination.

A child subjected to a parent in the "looking angry, looking really angry" escalation learns the signals well. Innocent baby sitters and also teachers become fair game until they learn how to scowl miserably enough to get control. An additional social problem is now added because parents and others don't like being forced to act mad and would rather not be around the child because they don't like the person they must become to keep control.

> It's not the money but the behavioral "cost" that makes this consequence work.

As described below in Reason No. 9, parents suffer most from the frequent punishment policy and the child may suffer less because he learns to adjust to people who will play the game he has learned and those who will not.

We all develop discriminations and act differently with different people. But when punishment is used, we do our best to avoid the punishing person altogether. The negative, critical, and threatening boss may have a reputation as a hard liner, but the employees will dodge her as much as possible and give no extra effort. Who wants to please *her*?

The relationship that develops is one in which two people only barely tolerate each other because they are forced to. A child would like to escape such a situation because of the possibility of being punished, and the parent would rather be away (at work, at meetings, or just out anywhere) because of the uncomfortable parental reactions that seem to be demanded by the situation.

Reason No. 9: Relatives will go home, parents will be left behind.

When "Get Tough" Uncle Harry finally leaves, Mom and Dad are left with the long-term side effects of punishments that have been too frequent and severe for the child to cope with. The child's solution may be to stop responding altogether or, at least, to respond as little as possible. The situation has produced a kind of success, the child *is* quiet. He is a very quiet child who believes his responses are likely to be pounced on with reprimands and corrections.

Even if the adults try a better approach when Harry leaves, the child may refuse to risk coming out of his shell. The biggest wish of this child is to get out—out of the room, out of sight or out of the house, if possible. Wouldn't we all rather dodge the punishment? With punishment you have to find your child; with praise, your child finds you.

> **With punishment, you have to find your child; with praise, your child finds you.**

Uncle Harry and Aunt Hazel will also leave behind other unintended effects. Often only a parent's opinion of her son or daughter is understood in punishment. The details of *why* you are so angry are smothered in your child's emotion, fear, and desire to leave. Combine the lack of understanding of the personal insult with the fear of risking any more punishment, and we are well on the way to losing all learning potential.

Left on their own with Harry's punishment advice, parents will be tempted to increase the punishment when the children don't seem to get the message. Many small children just can't seem to get on the right wavelength to figure out when Dad or Mom is "mad, acting mad, or *really* mad." Consistencies may be there, but the child just doesn't see them.

Punishment comes out of the blue and only tells a child one of the things he ought *not* to do, nothing about what *to do*. With so little to go on, the child could decide to ignore and forget these painful moments as soon as possible. We've all known a little Jessica or Juan whose mother increases reprimands, corrects, grabs, and sends him or her into confinement almost continually. Most of the time, if a child doesn't understand, he or she does whatever impulse comes to his or her mind while Mom becomes exasperated.

For the child who has become this timid, very minor events can act as punishments. Simply interrupting him when he intends to say something at dinner may silence him for the whole meal. A verbal snap from his sibling may accomplish the same thing.

It will require many isolated one-on-one moments with generous parents showing great tolerance and support to draw him out. For example, the parent might begin with a daily habit of games and puzzles and book reading in a special place alone with the child. Once the one-on-one sessions have been successful, the parents could try letting others back into the situation.

Reason No. 10: It leads to the ultimate punishment—divorce of parent from child.

When a puppy goes on the rug, we're tempted to swat him, but he doesn't learn much from that. And tomorrow it will be harder to teach him *anything* because he will be a little more timid—and harder to find!

A child, or an adult for that matter, could plan running away or, if running away is impractical, some other means of withdrawing. Of course a small child can be stopped, a teenager threatened, and a spouse could remind him/herself that there is more to lose. But no matter what good effect punishment may have in the short run, in the long run, you lose the victim.

That's why these strategies usually don't work on adults—adults can leave. But if the leaving option is not possible, then our victim may move on to other ways of escape, withdrawing to her room or to a special place or a corner of her mind to daydream.

A parent can anticipate what's on the mind of a child threatened with punishment and will usually decorate the punishment with, "As long as you live in this house..." or "You're not so big that I can't..." The implication is that the parent is counting on some other aspect of the situation to keep the child within range for deserved punishments. Either the doors must be locked, literally or figuratively, or the rewards from the parents are enough to compensate for the unhappiness.

A child may threaten to run away from home and the parent may appear to encourage that separation but this only intensifies the conflict and confusion because a child's home is his most important source of security.

Don't appear to be considering divorce from your children. This ultimate consequence is too disturbing and implies that your value of your child can be easily traded away. Your love and loyalty have a higher price tag, and they should not become part of bluffing or bargaining.

> **Your love and loyalty have a higher price tag and should not become part ot bluffing or bargaining.**

So why would anyone use punishment? With all these discouraging problems, you might wonder why some parents continue to use punishment. Even parent behavior should decrease when it is unsuccessful. So when their action (punishment) doesn't get the desired result, why don't they just quit?

The answer is that in the very short term, punishment produces results. If Mom punishes Fred for throwing sand while playing in the sand box, Mom's punishment behavior is rewarded by its immediate effect of interrupting Fred's bad behavior temporarily. Fred, a little more afraid and a little more confused, may start biting his nails. His stress habit will attract some attention, and we are creating an unpleasant routine supported by subtle short-term benefits. Mom gets a respite and Fred gets parental attention for his nail-biting. He has the added benefit of less blame, responsibility, or guilt because he "paid the price."

Correcting the course

Very young children don't usually show strong resistance to the parents' rules because they find natural gratification in many of the behaviors required. While growing from one to five, it's gratifying to succeed in dressing yourself, tying your own shoe, or in overpowering a spoon. In these cases the obvious usefulness of the task is a great advantage to the teacher.

But how quickly the worth of the task becomes debatable. After mastering the spoon, the next lesson is table manners. After successful dressing, the next lesson is proper selection and care of clothes. Now the parents must examine the reasoning behind their rules, and they are challenged to defend the reasoning. Arbitrary requests can put parents in the uncomfortable position of defending *their own* values. It's a small argument with a small person, but it is an ominous preview of the confrontations to come in the next 20 years.

> Eliminate rules no longer needed.

All parents from time to time neglect working out the reasons for their requests of their children. When surprised, they find themselves rationalizing in a desperate attempt to protect their authority and quell a childish rebellion.

Working out a justification can be more than a defense, it can be a review that will lead to eliminating rules no longer needed. Out of habit, a parent may continue to react and control behavior in an area where independence should replace inconvenient and unpleasant control.

Sometimes when a child is given a chore, a procrastination game can develop to provoke attention. Parents may nag, plead, and prod the child to do a chore all the time worrying that the "game" is being prolonged for the child's entertainment.

When parents feel reduced to unpleasant nagging, they may be tempted to blame the child not only for failure in the task, but for making them unhappy with the task of nagging. It's time to pause for a parent conference to look for a new strategy. The following conclusions and strategies might be good starting points for such conferences.

1. The behavior is too trivial to bother with.

Let's ignore it and eliminate a lot of unpleasant nagging and make more time for other kinds of conversation. This might apply to the way a child combs his/her hair, posture while watching TV, or the few scraps of food always left on the dinner plate.

2. The justification is off in the future.

When she/he starts noticing the impression others get from messy hair, sloppy posture, or wasteful habits, then we'll see a change. Let's wait for the expansion of his/her social circle to do it. Right now we can avoid sacrificing our family atmosphere by ignoring the problem.

3. The behavior is worth changing.

Let's think up a consequence that could work and stop all the nagging. From now on, anyone in the family showing terrible posture or wasting food has to put a penny in a jar on the kitchen table. Anyone completing a day without having to put in a penny may take ten cents from the jar (Mom or Dad pay off if the jar is empty).

4. The behavior really is worth changing, and it hasn't changed because the kids know they're getting through to us.

A reward is already working—it's the very nagging and pleading that we thought would solve the problem! It's time to pay close attention to ignoring this bad habit and looking for any time we can encourage little glimmers of good behavior that we hope will replace it.

Mom: "Let's all be in the clean plate club tonight!"
Kenny: "I hate green stuff."
Maria: "Me too!"
Mom: "It's good for you. Now eat up. I try hard to …"
Maria: "I'll take one bite." (Spoons up just enough to appear on a lab slide.)
Mom: "You too, Kenny."
Kenny: "This is ridiculous."
Mom: "Now Kenny, we have cookies for dessert."
Kenny: "I don't even like cookies."
Mom: "You know you like cookies …."

Later, in the planning session, blame sets in:

Dad: "That was a good dinner, but eating it was miserable!"

Mom: "Well, that's the way kids are, you know. I can't force them to eat."

Dad: "Kenny just does it to argue, and then they both eat what they want later. It's an attention-getting thing."

Mom: "It's their way of getting into the conversation."

Dad: "Maybe we should eat later, alone."

Mom: "That's a solution for us, but that won't make them eat any better. How about this idea: if you back me up on "no snacks," I'll just put out what we all should eat and that's it! They won't starve, they'll eat some of it, and maybe we can talk about something besides food at dinner."

Dad: "They'll whine for other stuff. We'll just have to ignore that."

Mom: "We tell them once that this is what we are having for dinner—that's it. I just won't have cookies and other stuff in the house. It won't always be convenient, but it's better than all this fighting to get them to   eat."

Dad: "Kenny will gripe all the way through dinner."

Mom: "We just have to bring up other topics like we would with visitors. He'll gripe at first but if we stick to it, he'll get used to eating what he wants of what is there. Just don't buy into the I'll-bet-you-can't-make-me-eat game."

Dad: "Me!? You're the one who ..."

Mom: "OK, OK. Never mind that, we have to be together on this. Remember we agreed to support each other in these sessions, not to go after each other."

Dad: "OK. Let's try it. As long as they're healthy, let them pick what they want from what we serve."

Mom: "We can even have a little dessert; just remember to bring up other subjects that they can be in on.

Dad: "And if it doesn't work we can always sell them."

Mom: "Ha, ha. Sorry, no buyers."

The strategy planned here may need modification later, and Mom and Dad will certainly need another session on other problems. The advantage of the session is that Mom and Dad are trying out a new way of handling a problem—not just reacting to each moment as it comes up—and they feel *they* are in control of what's going on.

5. The behavior is worth changing, not so much for reasons that benefit our child but because we would find it more pleasant and comfortable that way.

It's not for the child's sake, but for ours that we start the penny-jar procedure or the plan to ignore the bad behavior or the goal of looking for the good behavior to encourage. This may seem selfish but it can be valid. There's a place for selfishness in parenting:

Hannah: "Mom, why can't I stay out late and play every night? How can I get hurt in my own yard on some nights and not others? It doesn't make sense!"

Mom: "Well, on most of those nights you need the extra time for homework."

Hannah: "If I have my homework done, can I stay out?"

Mom: "You also need to rest sometimes."

Hannah: "Can I watch TV?"

Mom: "Well, I, ah, really meant for you to rest."

Sometimes the real justification for this kind of rule is that the parents want some evenings when they can have peace of mind and not worry about possible accidents and what's going on out there.

Mom: "I want you here with us some nights because I don't want to worry every evening."

This frank statement of parents' rights might not end the argument but at least Mom can feel more comfortable knowing she has a fair and above-board position.

Selfishness can be justified occasionally, but dishonesty is rarely justified. Parents should consider their reasons for rules even in the early years when children are only beginning to use rationality as a challenge. If five-year-old Randy can't go running and screaming through the house because it annoys Dad, telling him it is because nice boys don't do that changes the subject from an action (running) to a person (Randy). Without the consideration of Dad part, the message about Dad being annoyed gets mixed up with, "Dad thinks I'm not nice." The message sent is now much more than intended. We just wanted him to stop annoying us; he thinks we said he's a bad person.

> There's a place for selfishness in parenting, but dishonesty is rarely justified.

Avoid rules that only work once

Some planned consequences are better than others when it comes to their value in learning. A parental reaction may ignore the principle of repeated practice. "If you don't stop running through the house all the time, we won't go to the circus," or "We won't sign you up for soccer this year!"

Going to the circus is a single future event not likely to be repeated for some time and so is signing up for soccer. You're tempted to repeat the threat many times since the circus itself will only happen once. It's true that your child needs to learn that you should be taken seriously and that you mean what you say about the circus or about soccer, but the consequence is so far off that verbal decorations seem required because any outcome, way down the road, will seem weak at a distance.

> Any outcome, way down the road, will seem weak at a distance.

So after all the argument, you either give in and take the kid to the circus or you hold to your threat, don't take him to the circus, and admit you are giving no credit for the better behaviors. This says that, overall, he has been a bad kid. It's a one-shot consequence with no winners and little chance of a satisfactory outcome.

With a one-time consequence, parents are tempted to do a lot of talking in order to "milk" all the influence they can from the upcoming big event. The temptation is to hold out the possibility of punishment over the child for days or weeks.

> Allow yourself and your family the enjoyment of individual events without using them to limit bad behavior.

This situation is gloomy for the family and for the event when it finally comes. It's like holding off the enemy in battle with only one bullet; you have to do a lot of posturing, bluffing, and threatening. Once you use your bullet, you are an ogre for not allowing the circus or a patsy for giving in! And then the next day, you will need a new bullet and a new threat.

A better strategy is to allow yourself and your family the enjoyment of individual events without trying to use them to limit bad behavior or produce good behavior. Instead, choose a smaller event that can come up more frequently, something not so severe that has a positive side to emphasize. For example, instead of threatening to throw away all the toys that you have to pick up (an unmanageable and expensive threat with an "only once" character to it), you could designate a "daily toy closet" where any toys go that are still scattered after Mom has asked for them to be picked up. The closet will be opened only at a certain time and then the toys can be reclaimed by their owners. Any toy left for parents to pick up after that is put in the closet for the next opening.

This procedure has the advantage of being a consistent and repeatable consequence. It is not so severe as to make parents feel guilty and inconsistent, and it is logically related to the problem of too much mess or danger from too many toys being left out.

A very repeatable consequence makes it much easier to refrain from nagging. The repetition does the reminding. Nagging can stop and that will open the airways for more pleasant family talk.

Isn't adulthood great? Alternatives to punishment

A Mother and her daughter enter a supermarket and an accident occurs when her daughter pulls the wrong orange from a pile and 17 oranges gain their freedom. Mother grabs daughter and shakes and slaps her.

What do you do? Ignore it? Consider it a family affair—none of your business? Or do you advise the mother not to abuse her child? If she rejects your advice, do you insist or even call the police?

When do the rights of a daughter to fair and reasonable treatment begin? If the daughter is 19, are you more willing to interfere or even call the police? When do parents' rights to treat children as they please end? If 19 is clearly in the adult zone of protection, at what age should that protection start? If she were 16, is the punishment more justified? 10? 7?

For adults we look for other alternatives to handle mistakes; at what age do your children deserve that? The oranges avalanche was an accident, but the daughter should help pick them up——not just stand there and cry. Mom should help.

> **When do the rights of a child to fair and reasonable treatment begin?**

If you come to my house for dinner tonight and spill your drink at the table, you don't expect me to say: "Hey! What do you think you're doing? You're so clumsy! Now pay attention to what you're doing or I'll send you home!"

What nerve! Treating a guest like a child. What happened to "the benefit of the doubt?" You expect to be allowed to make amends; you expect me to belittle the problem, you even expect sympathy. I say, "Oh, too bad. No problem, I'll get a cloth." You say, "I'm sorry, let me get that. I'll take care of it." Isn't adulthood great?

Of course adults rightfully expect appreciation for their contribution, and, for mistakes, they expect to go unpunished and to have another chance. A good supervisor will recognize that fact and support good adult performance with positive reactions. Children deserve the same alternatives to punishment.

We all deal with unwanted adult behavior every day, but most of us have given up punishment of the straightforward kind, long ago.

> For adults, we look for alternatives to handle mistakes; at what age do your children deserve that?

The culture we live in continues to provide some punishment—"logical consequences" we sometimes call them—and the courts hand out punishments for the larger transgressions. But logical consequences and court sentences are usually long delayed and given only for repeated bad habits and big mistakes.

So with unwanted *adult* behavior, what alternatives to punishment do we use? Every day, adult mistakes receive *very kind* reactions. Even blowing your horn in traffic is considered too aggressive. Often we just allow the person to make amends, or we ignore the mistake altogether. If we control the situation, we might try to make it less likely he will repeat the mistake, "The boss should give better instructions, he should put up more signs about how to use the printer!" After more instruction, the boss may use warnings, "Anyone caught putting their sandwich in the printer will be ...." and then, maybe, a punitive consequence..

Along with making amends, we may try ignoring with the addition of a guarantee for good behavior. Since punishment has so many disadvantages anyway, let's go on to a more adult way of handling problems.

Alternative No. 1. Making amends.

This is the number one strategy adults use to handle bad adult behavior. When adults make a blunder, we would rather have the offender try again than punish him. At what age did you earn such consideration? Reactions to mistakes, by kids, teens, or adults, accidental or not, should start with allowing the blunderer to make amends. A child deserves the same respect. It is only fair to assume he is doing his best.

Grandma: (Sitting down to dinner) "Whoops. *Now* I know what I

forgot at the store—coffee! But we have juice, how about that?"
Mom: "Don't worry about it, juice is fine. We'll get the coffee tomorrow." (Mom minimizes the mistake.)
Grandma: "At least I'll get out the juice." (Grandma makes amends.)
Nealanni: "Hey! Mobby licked my spoon when I had it down there."
Grandma: "Don't use it now that the dog licked it! Keep your hands up! You're going back in your high chair if you don't have enough sense to ..."
Mom: (Interrupting) "Nealanni, get down and get yourself another spoon." (And then to Grandma) "I can get along without the coffee until tomorrow if you can. So no problem, right?"
Grandma: "What? Oh, ah, Yes, OK, OK. If I get a break on forgetting the coffee, I guess Nealanni gets a break, too. And, Nealanni, could you put the dog out while you're over there?"

Alternative No. 2: Ignoring.

Ignoring bad behavior eventually decreases it, especially if the child was acting up for the attention. If a parent can tough it out and hold back attention for the bad behavior, the child may go on to something else. The problem here is that in the short run, *more bad behavior* is likely rather than less. This bad behavior has been a part of a successful habit to get entertainment or attention from Mom and Dad. Now they plan to cut that off.

If the usual amount of acting up will no longer work, the child may escalate the volume! At the higher intensity, the parents may break the new rule and punish this outrageous behavior. If that quiets things down, the parents may return to the ignoring rule only to go back to punishment when the volume again reaches their pain threshold. The process builds up a new level of bad behavior. Escalation is a very common problem because the natural childish reaction to failure (to get attention) is to try harder.

> **The problem with ignoring is that in the short run, more bad behavior is likely, rather than less.**

If you use a vending machine at your job and one day it doesn't work, what do you do? Calmly give up? Or jab and yank on the coin return and bang on its little buttons. After your mini-tantrum, you look around for another solution to the problem—another machine or another choice. You know plenty of sources for what you want so you quit acting "like a kid" and go on to another solution.

Now what's available for your child when he finds his bad behavior no longer works his personal "vending machine?" Your child thinks, "If the usual volume isn't working, maybe I should add some really loud screams!" He's going to escalate, then look for another solution. What will he find? What can be added to ignoring so it will work?

Alternative No. 3: Ignoring plus.

This alternative adds a search for something good to the notion of ignoring the bad. As a tantrum subsides, a child finally begins to cast about for a new solution. What he finds and latches on to will depend on his parents' understanding of the outcome he is looking for. If the child is in need of attention, the situation will not be made better for the child if our strategy, overall, reduces the attention the child gets. We should make a mental note to *respond* to new behaviors *whenever* we plan to ignore unwanted behavior.

Ignoring the unwanted behavior *and* planning to encourage *specific and likely* successes will produce a better result. The message needs to be clear: "Now that's a good way to handle that!" "I liked hearing about your report on the Civil War battle. You're learning about interesting things." "I noticed you helped clear the table after supper. That's great!"

> **Ignore unwanted behavior and encourage specific and likely good behavior.**

There are advantages to watching for the successful behavior and providing good positive feedback when it occurs. This "catch 'em being good" notion can be particularly useful when you need the ignoring strategy for an unwanted behavior.

Practice and experience are the core of child development, but they only continue if positive consequences for successes keep coming. It can be tiresome and frustrating to a parent to let a child practice a task, foul it up, and do it again, and still offer encouragement, but it is essential.

Making a seven-year-old's bed is so much easier than coaxing him to try it and make a mess of it. Telling a ten-year-old girl what to wear is easier than sending her back to her closet to replace inappropriate clothing probably with more inappropriate clothing.

The situation can be particularly difficult when enthusiastic encouragement and reward must be provided for the first poor approximations of the ideal behavior, but the need for these reactions is crucial—this kind of practice is absolutely imperative. It would be nice if, after a little practice, children would go on to perform on their own, but we must provide continuous encouragement in order to enjoy continuous improvement. You need to be a rewarding parent just as you must be a rewarding spouse or friend.

Perhaps as a child you thought, "When I make mistakes everyone notices and I get in trouble, but a lot of times I do well, and nobody says a thing."

To prevent unwanted behaviors, parents need to "catch 'em being good," not just when the desired behavior occurs, but when a behavior in the right direction comes along.

Actions that are improvements and steps forward need the most encour-agement, recognition, praise, and reward. Be realistic about where to start the encouragement. In the "catch em being good" alternative, you need to start rewarding at the child's level now, and then move toward the improvements. A kid who stays in her room most of the time will not change if criticized, but may come out more often if she finds appreciation and activities she likes when she is in the family areas of the house.

Alternative No. 4: The cost of inconvenience.

Many little inconveniences, particularly those for older children and adults, may seem at first trivial, but when put into practice, they can be extremely effective. For example, putting a penny in a jar on the kitchen table every time Dad loses his temper may seem trivial for someone with plenty of pennies. But if the rule is followed, the inconvenience of having to stop, get a penny, go into the kitchen and put it in the jar can be a very effective consequence. It's not the money but the behavioral "cost" that makes this consequence work.

As a strategy for removing or reducing smoking behavior in adults, many psychologists use the principle of inconvenience. The heavy smoker is instructed to keep an exact record of his smoking throughout each day. He carries a little notebook wherever he goes and writes down the time, to the minute, when he takes out a cigarette, and the time he puts it out. He may be asked to note the situation as well, including who was with him and what he was doing.

Some psychologists also ask for the cigarette butts to be saved and brought in for counting. These tasks may not seem like consequences as we have talked about them so far, but they are consequences of a most useful type—they require time. A smoker may be too busy to make all those entries and save butts, so he may take a pass on having that cigarette at all.

Such a self-administered procedure requires a very cooperative and trust-worthy subject. I found the "cost-of-inconvenience" procedure more useful with smokers referred to me who have been told by their doctor that their health or even their life is at stake! They usually *want* the process to work and they can be counted on to try hard.

The procedure has not worked well when used on people who "feel they should cut down" or quit for the children's sake. These less motivated people need a stronger procedure than "the cost of inconvenience."

Children can be less motivated to change, but sometimes they can be enthusiastic about a record-keeping procedure. One mother reported that her 13-year-old son, Sean, continually disrupted the family by "checking things." On some evenings, he insisted on checking as many as 70 things before going to sleep. Sean checked to see if the back door was locked. He checked to see if the light was out in the basement. He checked to see if his pen was on his desk and if his dresser drawers were closed. Some of this would have been reasonable, but the situation got out of hand when he checked the same things for the fifth or sixth time in the same evening to his family's exasperation!

At first, his checking was examined for the possibility that it was an attention-getting behavior. Some progress was made by reducing Sean's parents' attention to the excessive checking and increasing conversation time before he went to bed.

The most effective procedure was beginning a record of every item checked, the time it was checked, the result of the check, and what could have happened if the item had been left unchecked. The procedure involved so much writing and decision-making that it was impossible to check 70 things each evening.

Because of the work and inconvenience of the procedure, Sean began to pass up checking items that were not so important and he made a special effort to remember the ones already checked, or he would look at his record, so that he didn't have to do it again. The number of times Sean checked things soon was down to a level that was only a little unusual instead of downright disruptive to the family.

The same principle of inconvenience can be used to increase a habit. For example, good homework habits can be influenced by how convenient it is to get started. If there is a place to do homework with little distraction and paper to work with, then we have a better chance of getting some homework done.

Dianne: "I'm not going to practice this stupid violin any more, it's too much trouble!"

Mom: "Just another ten minutes, then you can quit."

Dianne: "Phooey."

Dianne's practice is best done in intervals that keep frustration to a minimum, but once Dianne begins, Mom hates to let her quit because it's such a hassle to get her started again. Maybe Mom could do away with some inconveniences associated with Dianne's practice. She could help Dianne get out the music and set up the stand. Then while Dianne checks the tuning, Mom could turn off the TV and get everyone else out of the room. By removing the inconveniences, maybe Dianne would practice more frequently.

Mom: "Let's set up a special place for you. How about in our bedroom? We're never in there when you need to practice and it's away from the TV and your brother. You can leave your music stand out, and it won't be disturbed."

Dianne: "OK, but I still think all this practice is stupid."

We have not solved the violin problem by just finding a place to practice. Dianne is going to need more encouragement than that. Mom needs to visit the practice situation a lot, comment on the progress, and help the instructor make practice of interest to Dianne. But a place to practice easily, without frustrating start-up time, is a step toward making it all happen.

Alternative No. 5: Count-outs and time-outs.

Sometimes the bad behavior demands a reaction. We don't let adults get away with just anything, and children shouldn't be misled that anything goes either. What alternative is there when the mistakes should not be ignored, and making amends or hoping for opportunities for encouragement is not enough?

For young children, time-out is often a good solution. We all know the drill of putting the child on a chair or in his/her room for a little "cooling off" and isolation as a kind of punishment. The procedure can work well if the threats, arguments, and other verbal decorations that often precede the time-out can be kept to a minimum.

> **Many parents have found that starting the time-out, putting the child in the chair or room is the effective part.**

Mom: (Liz throws a toy at her sister.) "Liz! We don't throw toys. You could hurt someone. That's One!" (Liz throws again.) "Liz, that's *Two*."

Liz: "I don't *want* it!" (Liz throws again.)

Mom: "OK, that's Three," Mom takes Liz to the kitchen chair and deposits her there.

Mom is doing well. She doesn't talk much during the count which could lead Liz to act up and argue, Mom doesn't make a lot of threats, and she corrects Liz in a way that can be used frequently—no dramatic punishment that requires a big build-up.

How long should Liz remain in the chair? A very short time would be best. Many parents have found that starting the time-out, putting the child in the chair or room, is the effective part. Prolonged isolation will not be effective because the child will forget exactly what it was all about.

The situation will have changed so much after a long isolation that there will be no opportunity to practice anything right. Ten or 15 seconds is enough for two-year-olds, and one minute is enough for four, five, and six-year-olds. The message was sent when the prompt decision was made at the count of three (or ten, if that's the rule).

The same counting can be used for an ongoing behavior. Duncan starts rocking on his wobbly chair and Mom says, "Duncan, that's dangerous, stop it." If Duncan doesn't stop, Mom says, "Duncan, stop. That's dangerous. OK, that's one...two...three...." If Duncan is still at it at ten, Duncan goes to time out.

All five of these alternatives require effort, and some are downright hard work so make sure you eliminate any trivial behaviors from your rules before you start a plan. When Tim insisted on always using a fork to eat, even when it was chunky soup, his parents didn't like it but felt he should have the choice.

In their weekly planning session they agreed the use of a fork was unimportant and decided to make nothing of it. The "problem" was too trivial, and they decided *any* rule or reaction was too much. But when he hit his younger sister, they reacted strongly and used the time-out method.

Their different reactions to these very different behaviors keep the family atmosphere from becoming cluttered with unnecessary criticism of trivial temporary problems. Yet it's obvious that Mom and Dad care and will not tolerate bad behavior.

For example, Dustin always shows off and acts silly when company comes or the family goes visiting. He makes a fool of himself while watching his parents for their boiling point. He knows he can go further than usual and that Mom's and Dad's boiling points are much better predictors of real punishment than his own foolishness. Dustin has gained some control over the situation. True, it's miserable for everyone, but he likes being the focus *and* in control.

Two factors keep Dustin's parents from getting the upper hand. First, the punishment they might have in mind is too severe for frequent use: sending him off to his room for a long time (too rejecting), leaving him in the car when visiting (too dangerous), or swatting him (too hard on the social situation). So most of the time they use threats which only tell Dustin how far he has to go.

The second factor is that Mom and Dad lack specific definitions of what is right so they can encourage Dustin. They also need a definition of what is wrong so that if any reaction is to be used, it would happen because of what Dustin does, not for what his behavior *does to* his parents. Pinning down these definitions will put consistency back in the situation and return control to Mom and Dad.

The less severe "count-out-and-time-out" method is easier to use with specific definitions of expected behavior. For example, when the family goes on visits, Mom could use the car as a time-out for Dustin if she stays with him. If Mom is careful to react to Dustin's improvements as well, we may be on our way to a better experience:

Mom: "Dustin, if you act silly over at Aunt Hazel's, we're going to take a time-out in the car."
Dustin: "I'll be good."
Dad: "We're here. Dustin, why don't you carry in your cousin Keisha's present."
Dustin: (At the door) "Happy terrible birthday, Keisha!"
Mom: "Dustin, that's one."
Dustin: "Well, it is terrible."
Mom: "That's two and three. We're going back to the car, now!"
Dustin: "No, no, I'll be better. I'll play nice with Keisha."
Mom: "Sorry, the count's already done."
Mom: (After only one minute in the car) "OK, let's go back in and see what we're missing. When it's dinner time, I'll tell you and you can help me serve the salad we brought."
Dustin: "I'm going to *get* Keisha."
Mom: "Dustin, the rule is still the same: three counts and I'll have to take you to the car again—no extra chances."

Will Dustin be an angel the rest of the visit? Probably not, but Mom has a plan and Dustin is not going to be allowed to take over and continually ruin their visit. After a few visits, Mom and Dad's combination of time-outs and encouragements will win out or maybe

Dustin will have to be left at home with a (well paid) babysitter.

Could Mom and Dad use Dustin's nap time as a time-out? How can being sent to bed be used as a punishment at one time and sold as something the child should *want* at another? Putting a child to bed should not be used as a time-out.

The complication of negative reinforcement

The purpose of punishment, as everyone knows, is to reduce or eliminate bad behavior. We have discussed the pros, cons, and alternatives to that style. Another, even more common style, is negative reinforcement. It is not punishment for mistakes; it's punishment for *failing* to do the right thing! The threat of a consequence for failing to meet someone's expectations is a common experience in a routine day.

> **The threat of a consequence for failing to meet someone's expectations is a common experience in a routine day.**

Why do I make dinner for the kids at the same time every night, use their favorite plate, prepare only certain foods? Is it because they watch for their chance to support my "good" behavior? No, the answer here usually begins, "Well, if I didn't do that, the kids would complain and make a lot of trouble."

If it's the *lack* of performance that would produce bad consequences from the kids, it's negative reinforcement from them. As long as Mom avoids unwanted dinner delays or unwanted food and doesn't disappoint her little masters, *she avoids* their nasty behavior. Children can also use negative reinforcement. For example, if the children treat each other right, *they can avoid* Mom's mad reaction.

The difference between regular punishment and negative reinforcement is important. Regular punishment, in its consistent form, is painful, but easy to understand. "If I do the wrong thing, I'll get bad consequences." Negative reinforcement is also painful, but the rule is more obscure: "If I fail to do the right thing, I'll get bad consequences."

Mom: "Zack, did you pick up your toys?"
Zack: (Watching TV) "Not yet."
Mom: "Did you put your dirty clothes in the laundry?"
Zack: "No."
Mom: "How about the mess in the living room?"
Zack: "OK. As soon as this is over."

Mom: "Take those dishes out, too."

Zack: "OK." (Remains an intimate part of the couch.)

Mom: (She's used no punishment up to here, but now she reacts to Zack's *lack* of action.) "Zack, I have had it! Now turn off that TV and get these things cleaned up!"

Zack: "OK, OK. Don't have a cow about it." (Mumbling)"Gee, who knows when you're gonna blow up, anyway?"

Mom: "What was that?"

Zack: "Nothing."

Part of Zack's and Mom's problem is that Mom's strategy is negative reinforcement. If Zack fails to perform (enough times) and Mom repeats her request without success (enough times) then Mom gets mad. Mom may also support and compliment Zack if he cleans things up, but Mom's exasperation limit and Zack's fear of her are the main factors at work in the situation.

At times, the distinction between regular punishment and negative reinforcement may seem like a word game. Could we simply say that Mom threatens regular punishment for Zack's sloppiness? She could use that strategy, lock up the toys when she sees them left out, for example. But the punishment she uses is triggered by the lack of behaviors and occurs at a non-specific time. Zack is tempted to continue to procrastinate, delay, and test the limits while Mom is driven to using "mad" as a motivator.

Negative reinforcement does not produce a happy situation. If most of your everyday activities are to avoid someone's flak, you're probably unhappy with him or her (we all know who we mean!):

Dad: "Did you take the car in today?"

Mom: "Yes, it just needed a tune up."

Dad: "Great, thanks for getting it over there; that takes a lot off my mind." Dad used the positive reinforcement idea, but in the next minute he slips to negative reinforcement:

Dad: "Did you get the little dinners I wanted for lunches?"

Mom: "Didn't go by the store after work."

Dad: "Hey, how am I supposed to work all day without lunch?" (Here's a reprimand as negative reinforcement for Mom's failure to do the right thing.)

Mom: (Borrowing from Zack) "OK, OK, don't have a cow over it. I'll get them tomorrow and I'll make something good for you to take in the morning." (Mumbling) "Gee, beam me up, Scotty!"

Dad: "What was that?"

Mom: "Oh, nothing."

Children have a better chance finding positive reinforcements everyday because parents and teachers know kids have to be encouraged. But negative reinforcement is probably the more common childhood experience even if it is a less popular term. It occurs when a behavior is used to *avoid* punishment: Make your bed or Mom will be mad. Do your homework or the teacher will embarrass you in front of the class. Be home on time or Dad will be furious. Even though the intention is to motivate, it sounds like—and it is—a threat.

For the child, the situation requires an effort to avoid the threatened outcome. He might want to escape the situation altogether; he could try to run away but usually he will try to deal with it.

> **It's similar to a marriage held together by one spouse hopping from one errand or task to another trying to keep the other spouse from getting mad.**

We're all familiar with the dark cloud of negative reinforcement produced by past bosses or parents and the escape we, at times, wished for. We recognize it when we hear someone say, "Well, if I *didn't* do it, I'd get so much criticism..." If your day is filled with such efforts to stay out of the line of fire, you may have leaving on your mind.

If most of what your child does is an effort to avoid punishment or embarrassment, he or she will find it hard to be happy but won't have the resources to leave.

It's similar to a marriage held together by one spouse hopping from one errand or task to another trying to keep the other spouse from getting mad. This unhappy situation may last for years, and it doesn't make a pleasant home or school environment either.

Even with the threat removed, a child (or spouse) may be afraid to risk ignoring a threat actually removed long ago. It will take some time and courage to test the new situation.

So here's a possible resolution: Every day, find something to compliment, appreciate, and support. Translate some old negative reinforcement into its flip side—the positive encouragement for what should be done instead of the criticism for failures. Gush a little, even if you have to be a little corny. Tell your child you noticed when he makes a successful effort—cleaned up some dishes—said something nice to his brother—got ready for school without complaints about clothes and lunches.

This "behavioral smile" is contagious; the kids are likely to copy your effort and the new style will recycle through the family. Keep it up—even a spouse can pick up the habit!

The work of being a parent

So it may not be that parents have reduced authority and power in these tough times, but rather that they need to recognize that there is a price to power, sometimes requiring a trade-off of personal conveniences in order to keep a rebellious child-teen progressing in the right direction.

Allowing a child to make amends, using count-outs, or ignoring and looking for something good—*all* require diligent effort. Contrary to the easy magical advice from aunts, uncles, and some professionals, being a parent can be hard work. So make sure you eliminate rules concerning trivial behaviors before you start any of these plans.

Aunt Hazel and Uncle Harry won't be satisfied with these alternatives, but they also would be disappointed in the results of punishment because neither punishment nor these alternatives will produce the instant change they want.

EXERCISE
A planning session agenda

Planning sessions have a dangerous tendency to turn into general gripe sessions. Although complaining can be therapeutic, parents often jump around from one problem to another without concluding a plan for any particular one.

So a planning session needs an agenda that will focus on planning parental reactions to a particular situation. The session should also produce an overall understanding of what is going on when the specific problem is encountered.

The purpose of this exercise is to do a complete "walk through" of a problem you identified in the earlier exercises. You may not always need such a complete analysis, but for the purpose of becoming alert to the possible aspects of behavior, this exercise will include all the steps.

First select a behavior from your priority list on page 97. This will be the problem under discussion in this session:

Item 1: Fill out a Behavior Chart as you did on page 67.
Use the chart at the end of this book. You will not yet have a record

of the behavior as described in the last part of the chart but put down your own observations as you remember them to answer these questions.
1. What would be an objective description of the behavior?
2. What happens next?
3. Where would you place possible blames and/or credits?
4. At what age would you expect an average child to do what you are hoping will be done in this situation?
5. How could you allow more practice?
6. When do things happen? (Keep a record.)

Item 2: Review this checklist for consequences as you consider possible reactions to the behavior. Pose each of the following questions in the planning session:

1. Is the problem big enough to bother with?

Remember even a "No" here should indicate a strategy—a strategy to eliminate nagging your child or yourself about the problem.

2. Am I attempting too much at one time?

A tempting pitfall in parenting is to try to make too many changes at the same time. Don't attempt to control eating, piano practicing, bedmaking, and doing homework all at once. Concentrating on too many plans leads to mistakes and too much "policing." Think small. Begin with one rule at a time.

3. Can I influence the behavior in an easier way?

Some worrisome behaviors can be reduced simply by engineering the environment. For example, you could set aside a special kitchen drawer of safe utensils for a son or daughter's cooking projects. This may be easier than worrying about the child's finding and handling dangerous or fragile tools.

4. Have I thought of all the consequences that could be maintaining the behavior?

What usually happens when the "bad" behavior occurs and what happens next? What usually happens if she performs correctly? If you select a new consequence, how should you set up the practice?

5. Is it a one-shot consequence?

A one-shot consequence is a promise of something good or

threat of something bad in the distant future as a consequence for a *present* behavior problem. Whether a threat or promise, it has the same disagreeable characteristics: it is not repeatable and tempts the parents to use repeated threats and will probably be somewhat arbitrary in the end. And then the next day what should you do? Start a new threat?

6. Is the consequence too severe?

You want something that can be used easily and repeatedly. So don't make plans when you're still angry over a mistake. Paying attention to only bad behavior won't help. Plan to reward good behaviors reasonably and react to bad ones reasonably.

7. If ignoring is the plan, are you prepared to handle your child's response to the deprivation?

If tantrums are ignored, what will attract your attention?

8. Is my expectation reasonable?

Even if it is reasonable, it may still be much more than your daughter has ordinarily been doing. She was used to nibbling and now you fill the plate and tell her no dessert until she finishes. Remember to start where *she* is, not where you *wish* her to be.

9. Is the consequence too weak?

What can be done if your child just doesn't seem to care about the new consequence? It could be that you are not sticking to the rule and he really doesn't *have* to care. Or possibly he has too many freebies available (If I can't go out, I'll watch TV!).

10. Am I starting with a behavior simple enough to ensure that rewards can occur—even on the first day?

Item 3: Review this Checklist for Alternatives to Punishment.

1. Could I use the adult reaction to mistakes, making amends?
2. Is it possible to first try *ignoring*?
3. Before going on to harder work, could I model the good behavior for my child?
4. Have the other possibilities presented in this chapter been considered?: "Catch 'em being good," "changing the convenience" of the behavior, and "count-outs and time-outs."

Chapter 7
Tips about dealing with "almost-grown-ups"

The teenager stage begins at about age 10 in the United States. An overload of information about sex and drugs and cynical attitudes about people, school, and the future are in abundance by the time a middle schooler heads for high school.

The teenage stage ends when the young adult develops the self-confidence of a grown-up and shows considerate and thoughtful behavior even when he is near his parents! Without some confidence-building from parents along the way, this adult stage could be delayed until our "teenager" passes 30, as many have observed.

Rule No. 1 for a teenager almost on his own

How can parents hang on to a little sanity for themselves and still help their child-teen survive the upcoming critical decade? The first step begins with an understanding that the greatest need of a teen is to be liked. Not just by peers, but by family also. Love is not enough.

Rule No. 1, then, is watch for chances to bolster confidence and avoid the straight diet of advice, quick fixes, and new demands. Skipping this rule about compliments is easy to do because teens, like many of us, don't handle compliments well and feel an obligation to brush off any positive remark. Parents may think their efforts have no effect, but parents who find the best in their teens, will establish confidence and self-esteem even though their teens may not show their appreciation until they pass 20.

In a family, all attitudes recycle.

An important caution in showing how much you like your teen is that most teenagers also harbor a great fear of embarrassment. I know the worst dread of my school day was that the teacher, the bus driver, a friend, or an adversary would embarrass me.

Therefore apply rule one carefully and not too thick to avoid that embarrassment that would keep a teen from trying new things. When you were a teenager, did you allow yourself to try out all your abilities and risk the practice needed to learn a new skill? The fear continues at home too. So while you are bolstering your teens' confidence, be sure to avoid embarrassing them.

"Practice what you want to become" is a useful result of the bolstering confidence rule. Your child-teen will practice the habits you support. Keep the pessimism low and the encouragement high.

> In a family, all attitudes recycle.

The goals are to raise a teen to become a competent adult, to have all the family members *enjoy* the family, and to remain close friends when the job is done.

Dr. Gloria Wright who works with men suffering from depression says that often the root of the problem is unfulfilled longing for acceptance from Dad. She notes that every man longs for the day his father says, "You're the son I always hoped you would be."

Daughters have the same feelings I am sure, and Mom's acceptance is just as important as Dad's. But Dads may hold back on the gushier stuff just when it's needed most. Often called upon to be the heavy (Wait 'till your father gets home!), Dads sometimes miss the opportunity when pride and admiration are in order.

We Dads sometimes find giving praise difficult, but when thinking of how to show appreciation for a Father's Day gift, for example, we need to gush a little: "What a great idea! I've been thinking about one of those for a long time. Right on target. Thank you!"

Holding back can turn a child's longing into frustration and then to cynicism about pleasing Dad. Once that stage is reached, the turn-around will take a real effort: "You're getting very good at soccer." Or, as one father said when his daughter complained about how long she had spent making a very impressive science project: "It's great. People won't ask how long it took; it's so good they'll ask who did it."

Compliments are a highlight for any child even if he or she doesn't show it. Parents may think they are having little effect, but remember that kids often feel obligated to act cool and pretend that praise doesn't make a difference. Don't be misled. The reaction may be bland, but the long-term accumulated effects will contribute to a great relationship.

Magical thinking and how to correct it

The signers of the Declaration of Independence knew the value of both education and hard work. It was clear to them that effort and learning in school would be rewarded in work and life.

Today, many students believe they might "make it" even to enormous financial success just by luck, or by skill in sports, or by knowing the right people. It's a possibility promoted by lotteries, TV, and the news.

So without incentives to focus attention on the learning at hand, many students become victims of magical thinking about success, and they develop unrealistic views of how "luck" will carry them through.

We adults also become victims of magical thinking. That's why we now approve of lotteries and other gambling, but our grandparents wisely, I think, did not.

We sometimes engage in magical thinking not only about a financial windfall, but also about our students: "The ones with the 'right stuff' will always do well." "The kids will work harder at school if parents take a harder (more punitive) line, or if the teachers would enforce more strict (more punitive) rules."

Faced with a student's failure and rebellion, a parent is tempted to criticize and punish. But the solution is on the positive side—with incentives, praise and respect expressed in concrete ways that raise self-esteem and confidence.

Some may object that gushing with praise is the wrong solution, but the danger for most of us is not in overdoing it, but in doing it at all. Encouragement and parental support involve a commitment of time and attention.

Representatives in Congress with their large salaries and teachers on the line with their modest ones should pause before objecting to the notion of rewarding students. This may be the most important part of the teaching and the parenting job. Few of us work for nothing.

I know it seems like a lot of trouble, and we all wish students would work just for the love of it and learn just for the love of learning, but most will not. We are a goal-oriented species with ambitions that can go astray. We need daily course corrections from generous positive feedback.

If a student behaves badly in school, we often say it is his fault—he is rebellious, aggressive, too distracted, or not very smart. In a recent study focused on the ways we explain children's problems in school, school psychologists listed the causes of these school problems as:

1. The material was not appropriate,
2. The teacher was not doing a good job of teaching,
3. The organization of the school was wrong,
4. The parents of the child were not supportive, or
5. Something about the child was amiss—motivation, innate ability, or emotional disturbance.

When teachers were asked to think back about the children they had taught, they attributed 85 percent of the problems to number 5, the children themselves. It's partly true of course but it attributes the problem to the factor that is most unchangeable.

Attention to the daily frequent successes with encouragements and compliments produces the best long-term progress.

Your "almost grown-ups" need your perspective

As a 10-year-old acts like a teenager and a teenager acts like an alien, the adult perspective sets a standard for the kids and nearly everything needs frequent review. Just when you think the parenting job would get easier, it's time to pick up the pace of accommodating change.

Most children enter middle childhood by hesitant steps, feeling threatened, lacking self-confidence, and with lots of questions and fears. They need your support "at the ready" in the form of respect, recognition, praise, and encouragement. All these are better than money or treats. And they are crucial for the essential feeling of self-worth. Self-worth is a particularly elusive feeling for children and teenagers.

What do your kids still need from you?

"It's amazing how Duncan has taken to helping in the kitchen! He's five and yet he can really do things! He made his own scrambled egg the other morning. I told him how impressed I was, and he made one for me!"

What fun it is to impress your parents! Duncan loves to help with cooking, doing a little on his own, and having his parents say how great he is.

Since parental approval is such an emotional high point, it is a shame some parents often begrudge their children "too much" reward. Reward and reinforcement are terms that may sound too mechanical because the words imply a contrived influence on behavior. But the most frequent reward children receive is the admiration and appreciation expressed by parents. Parents who are generous with these "rewards" are more effective.

Many are still uncomfortable with the notion that selfish benefits are required to get children to do the right thing. "They know it's good for them! They should be glad to have a good home and a chance to learn and advance!"

Isn't this the way we all feel sometimes? It seems unbelievable that kids would pass up an opportunity for personal growth or fail to contribute to the family out of appreciation for the care they get.

It's children we're talking about, of course. Adult employees who are asked to work a little longer or teachers asked to carry a larger load deserve rewards for their extra work. And our boss who expects something for nothing just doesn't understand our personal economic situation!

As a matter of fact, the higher you go, the more reward is expected for any effort—managers and school principals don't feel respected unless they make more money. Corporate officers and members of Congress worry that lower salaries for them would bring in people less competent than themselves, they say. And CEO's demand golden parachutes of stock options so they will have the "proper incentive" to do a good job up there on top. So the higher-ups commonly get more money and appreciation while both money and appreciation become scarce lower down.

The arbitrary and sometimes prejudiced distinction between what is appropriate and fair for adults and what children should expect often confuses our reactions to family problems. Whether the issue is a reprimand for a mistake or an incentive for progress, the wise parent can gain a new perspective from the adult vs. child debate. What would be appropriate if your child's problem behavior was exhibited by an adult? For example, Adam at age seven continually disrupts dinner with loud, inappropriate noises, giggles, and comments. You might ask, "What would we do about an adult, say Uncle George, if he acted this strangely?"

For Uncle George, you might first try to calm him down by bringing up a different subject of interest to him. We all know that the person most in danger of becoming obnoxious is the one who is left out, bored, or has nothing to do. The conversation should include Uncle George if we want a pleasant and comfortable guest, and perhaps the same goes for little Adam.

If that didn't work, you might try a reprimand on Uncle George and the same might be used on Adam. Beyond that, we would probably abandon the positive reinforcement idea, and our view of the Uncle George problem and the Adam problem would become very different. Uncle George would probably be tolerated with a mental note not to have him back. Adam, on the other hand, would probably be punished, sent to his room perhaps, or even snatched from his chair for a little stern squeeze. That might get results for the short run, but as experienced parents know, the dinner situation would be ruined, everyone would be mad, and Adam, unlike Uncle George, *will* be back.

Adam might do better if he got some adult treatment. Step One for Adam might be to have him eat by himself earlier the next evening. Then when he comes back to the family table, we might use the Uncle George treatment for Step Two—a conversation at his level and interest. If there is more trouble we could repeat Step One of having Adam eat earlier and then Step Two of having him back for another try. How many times? Probably until he gets it right since we can't just send him off (Uncle George probably won't take him!).

> **Parents who are generous with their admiration and appreciation are more effective.**

Another approach to looking for reasons for Adam's behavior is to ask, "If Adam were not behaving badly, what would be available to him and what would be our reaction?" Is there any suggestion or incentive for Adam to show any *particular* behavior? This approach leads us back to the change-the-subject-to-fit solution.

But when Dad and Mom sit down to dinner, they have stories to tell about their day at work and elsewhere. Adam has stories also, but he's not as skillful with language, and it's hard for him to break in if he doesn't get some patient consideration. It's difficult for Adam if Mom reports on a conversation at work and Dad comments on the TV news and Mom responds with her description of the newspaper report on the same story and Dad says...and Mom says...and Adam gets in the conversation only by acting up.

The adult conversation might only recognize Adam's presence with, "Sit up in your chair," "Eat your peas," "Don't make bubbles in your milk," and the ever-popular, "Now look what you've done!" Which is *exactly* what Adam wanted everyone to do—look at what he was doing! Is this how he gets his share of the dinner conversation? Uncle George would chime in on the news report or Mom's work experience, but Adam is not up to that and so he has to settle for negative attention—better than no attention—and he probably hopes the whole situation will soon be over.

This notion of deserved attention might also apply to a child in a class-room. Danielle's problem comes up in the lulls in classroom activity. You might say that Danielle, like Adam, doesn't know enough to busy herself without getting into trouble, but another way to put it is that, for Danielle, the opportunities for good behavior are not obvious enough for her. If she's a first or second grader you wouldn't expect her to know what to do. She lacks practice and if the class is large, the rewards for "acting right," even if she knows what that means, are likely to be infrequent and the benefits obscure.

It takes a fine teacher or mother to be able to catch Danielle or Adam being good and provide the encouragement and attention they need. If the teacher can hold to the view that the problem is a lack of something in the classroom that Danielle needs, not an unchangeable problem inside Danielle, she can improve just like Adam.

Price Tags on Behavior.

In a more perfect world, everyone would do the right things for the right reasons. We wouldn't need special incentives such as pay checks, bonuses, benefits, or parents using the right reaction. The work would be done because we all know it needs to be done.

But in the real world, all dieters, regular working folks, and exercisers know that free-floating motivation is hard to maintain. We either keep going in order to avoid the negative reinforcement, or some positive reinforcement is in the offing. As a matter of fact, if you only encounter negative reinforcement in a situation, such as a job, you're probably already planning to make a change.

"Quit treating me like a child!": Eight years old and going on 25!

You don't have to carry around a bag of money and candy to keep the kids shaped up. You carry around yourself and, for the most part, that's enough. An honest expression of appreciation, praise, and encouragement can be very effective *if* done thoughtfully.

Social rewards are so easy to give that they are often given in an offhand manner—forgotten when they are most needed, thrown in when they send the wrong message. A rigid plan of reactions to your children would not be good either, but a continuous flow of casual attention has the danger of drawing attention to troublesome behaviors and unimportant activities, making bad behavior out of what was, at first, trivial.

> Mom: "Careful with the eyes on the teddy bear, they could come off."
> Arial: "They could come off?"
> Mom: "They're just sewn on."
> Arial starts to finger the eyes of the teddy bear.
> Mom: "I told you to be careful. Just leave them alone."
> Arial: "They won't come off, see?"
> Mom: "Don't do that! They'll come off."

Whether Arial or her mom turns out to be right about the teddy bear, the situation is now a confrontation, and if I were the teddy bear, I'd be nervous. Mom started fixing a problem before she had one, and now she has one. Let's have her try another situation:

> Arial: "I'm gonna sit on a regular chair at supper."
> Mom: "OK."
> Arial: "Really. I'm big enough." (Here's a hint that we are into an attention-getting game. Why didn't Arial just sit when she got the "OK" from Mom?)
> Mom: "Uh huh."
> Arial: (Sits on a regular chair) "I can't see from here." (Waits, but gets no reaction) "I want my old chair back, but I want it over here with a pillow."
> Mom: "OK. I'll help you move it." (Now Mom reacts to a reasonable request.)

Mom's bland reaction to Arial's first idea provided no spotlight for Arial's seating problem. She tries something that's not satisfactory, and then something that is. All the time Mom does a good job by keeping this demand at the level of importance that it deserves.

Your social rewards, then, deserve close attention at times. You can't police yourself every moment, watching every move of your child and every word you say, and it would be an inhuman situation for anyone who did. But when you are considering a *specific* behavior of your child, always consider the role your social attention plays—for good or ill.

Sophisticated adults give social attention and approval in subtle ways that can send mixed (and mixed up) messages to a child. We use a nod of the head or lift of an eyebrow or a curiously phrased remark such as, "I guess you finally got that right." Or, "All right, you're better than last week." "You bet." "Oh, right, what a great job that was!" It's hard to put into print exactly what these remarks mean without describing inflections and pauses and tone of voice.

Adults have a lot of practice in using and hearing such subtleties. But a child, not yet grown up, hasn't learned all the details of sarcasm or understatement and the meanings these details convey.

Make sure your sophistication doesn't get in the way when you are trying to support your child. Send your message clearly; be frank and outspoken when you like what has been done: "Yes, that's good." "That's what I like you to do." Say it loud enough; say it simply; let him or her know you mean it.

Even later when the eight-year-old is approaching 25, the habit of an occasional clear message of admiration should not be neglected. Most of us didn't end up doing exactly what our parents had hoped for. I know my three children all took surprising directions. But you don't want home to be a place to avoid because they're usually reminded of what they're doing wrong! Visits become rare when that habit sets in.

Fat cats and matching funds.

Cats seem to be one of the best animals at taking human care for granted. Good food, housing, and a warm pillow, and they can ignore you for days. A child growing from age two to 12 may sometimes take a similar attitude. During a moment of rebellion, a child can act on the false idea that she is perfectly capable of making it on her own. Like the cat, she has been misled by a family situation that provides most of the essentials of life free and with no fanfare. You too could make it on very little if room, board, clothing, medical, and educational needs were free!

The fat cat problem develops from too few demands on the child to care for herself and to contribute to the family as she acquires more ability. As the teenage years loom not too far ahead, it's time for more realistic responsibility. But when you give more responsibility you also need to be aware of successes and say so.

A matching funds arrangement, along with a grad-uated allowance can help a money situation when a growing teen makes more financial demands. Allowances are the major source of income for children and the teenagers they aspire to be. A graduated allowance pays off a variable amount depending upon the activities of the child/teen. It includes a guaranteed allowance unrelated to performance and provides responsibilities for the child to earn additional amounts gradually over the week. Each time the child finishes a task, it is recorded on a chart. Each task has a value and the accumulated amount is paid off at the end of the week.

The possible increase in allowance need not be more expensive for the family budget. As money accumulates, it doesn't all have to be spent on her amusement and stomach! Consider a matching funds program for clothes, for example, where parents may provide most of the funds but for some items, the child contributes to the cost from his or her earnings.

Concrete rewards may also be needed when laziness has become so habitual and resistance to change so strong that we need contrived rewards to make even small steps in progress. For example, to improve the homework habit, you might adjust the weekly allowance according to the amount of homework done. Some allowance is coming to the child anyway, but important school work needs to be done, so the real world might as well start right here—the work and the pay go together.

> An incentive for doing hours of homework for a child who can't stick with it for 10 minutes is doomed to failure.

Set the limits, both minimums and maximums, so that you can't be cornered into an unreasonable position such as allowing *no* money if no homework gets done or having to pay too much if all the homework is done. You will want to keep it simple, but without stated limits you'll be tempted to give out undeserved money or have to refuse to pay up for a sudden burst of activity.

It will be better to set limits at the beginning—say a $3 minimum and a $10 maximum, adjusted upwards for age. The practice is the most important thing going on in the child's life, so let's give practice some importance. We guarantee the minimum by saying, "The $3 is for every week, but I'll add a dollar for each night your homework is all done, and two extra for a whole week of successful homework nights." You could tie the definition of "homework done" to pages of workbooks, teacher assignments, or time spent on homework each night.

With this amount of structure, you'll avoid being an ogre who won't give any allowance, and you'll avoid extravagant payoffs. After a few weeks, you may want to add special incentives for some subjects or change the definition of "homework done," or add an extra pay increase for special efforts. All rules are subject to change.

One of the keys to success in using incentives is to make very reasonable requests, especially at first. These requests should not be based on what *should* be done but on what *has been the usual*. An incentive for doing hours of homework for a child who can't stick with it for 10 minutes is doomed to failure. Start at the level of the child now, establish his/her confidence, then the requests can be increased.

On day one, you want to guarantee that you will get an opportunity to use your incentive! Plan it for a performance not only within your child's ability but within his/her inclination as well. For example, you might ask that only one page of a workbook assignment be completed before a half-hour of TV is approved. The payoff is so attractive and the price tag so small that success is likely. With little successes "in the bank," you can start a progression toward the amount of homework required before the reward is available. The increments should be small enough to allow a smooth and easy increase in effort.

> **Chores are useful in building self-esteem and respect.**

You must be careful when selecting "less logical or materialistic" rewards such as TV because they are usually not a natural benefit of the behavior and the time will come when your children will be out on their own and faced with less generous people. This means that your encouragement, admiration, and praise must remain a major part of the rules even when concrete rewards are used.

Your reactions must continue to send the message of the importance and usefulness of the activities you support. You hope that your target objectives are likely to be supported outside the family in a way that is at least enough to keep your child on the right path.

What can they *do* now? The activities that other people support and believe important are probably the same as yours. Chores such as washing the car, mowing the lawn, painting, cooking, and shopping are some of the easy ones. A young person usually values the same activities but it may not be "in" to say so.

The child's usual attitude toward chores should not mislead parents. Chores are useful in building self-esteem and respect. Even children who moan and complain when asked to pitch in, still grow a little when they *do* pitch in. Everyone wants to feel competent and able. So when you ask your child to do chores, take heart in the fact that the advantage goes far beyond getting the chores done. As a matter of fact, the boost in the child's self-respect may be the most important outcome!

Now as you allow your offspring into adult activities, remember to include the fun as well as the less desirable parts of the job. When washing the car, she should get to use the hose as well as scrub the wheels. When shopping for food, he should be allowed to pick out a goody as well as get the soap.

One last caution concerning the first efforts to support good behavior: the proof of a little success is in the daily and weekly changes, *not* the immediate reactions of the kids. Remember kids can be very pessimistic about your power. The pessimism may come from their own feeling of powerlessness as well as a desire to discourage you from trying to influence them! Don't buy it. The proof of change is in the longer term reactions and adjustment.

A second related tactic of your kids may be to belittle the consequence as too weak to do any good. The power of consequences is in their accumulated numbers. Use small compliments and encouragement: "You're running the laundry through by yourself? You really are growing up!" or "Gerry, why don't you call in the pizza order, you're getting so good on the phone."

Every penny in the bank adds up—don't be talked out of it, just say (or think), "Let's see how it goes."

"Mom, all the kids are going!" Beware the stampede technique.

It's easy to slip out of your adult perspective when dealing with frantic children. Everyone is in a hurry, even the kids, and the combination of the rush and outrageous arguments of a child can lead to lamented reactions. In Chapter 1 on listening, one of the cautions is to keep the pace of conversation slow enough for a child to keep up and not resort to defensiveness.

With older children, parents can be the ones rushed into mistakes by kids who have learned that picking up the pace and pressure can have advantages. Questions asked with a lower voice and a slower pace can exasperate a child, but that's better than heading into dangerous situations: "When did you say you will be home?" (asked at a deliberately slow pace), or "Wait a minute, whose parent is going to drive and when will they pick you up?"

> Ramon: "Dad, Todd and his brother are going to the beach for the weekend. They asked me, can I go?"
> Dad: "Ah, Who did you say is going?"
> Ramon: "Todd and, ah, some of his family. Dad, he's waiting on the phone!"

Dad: "Well, I think we should talk about it; Todd's parents are going?"

Ramon: "Dad, I don't know who all is going, can I go or not?"

Here's a good place for Dad to slow the pace. We would all want more details before sending a 12-year-old off for the weekend and Dad's not going to get them with Todd waiting on the phone. Why is there no time to go into details? Caution, the answer may be that someone would like to avoid the details.

Dad: "Tell Todd you'll call him back in a few minutes."

Ramon: "He needs to know now! Can I go or not?"

Dad: "Not. Unless we can talk."

Ramon: "OK, I'll tell him I'll call back, but if I miss it, it's your fault."

Making time for yourself in moments of demands has advantages beyond just getting details. Dad needs a moment to pay attention to his intuition and instincts about Ramon's proposal. Exactly what is it that's bothering him about this request and how can he deal with it?"

Ramon: "OK, I'm off the phone, what's the problem?"

Dad: "Ramon, I need to talk to Todd's parents before you can go."

Ramon: "Dad, I'm not just a kid anymore."

Dad: "True, but you can't go with just Todd and his brother."

> **Why is there no time to go into details? Maybe someone would like to avoid the details.**

Is this the end of the argument? Probably not, but Dad knows what is reasonable, and he's not going to be stampeded into a bad decision because someone's waiting on the phone. If Ramon misses his chance because Todd has to go and his parents aren't there or have no time to talk, maybe it's just as well. It's not a pleasant family moment, but better than a weekend of worry or worse.

Bring in the reinforcements

Would-be teenagers are a new challenge for parents with or without partners. The parenting job is fast changing from child-rearing to adult-rearing. Expanding moments of separation become more apparent and the paradox of *keeping* control while also *giving it away* creates tough times for all parents.

Single parents have many disadvantages in rearing "almost adults" but they have one advantage: a consistent set of rules and reactions not compromised by a second authority. Nevertheless, as every single parent knows, other adults still chime in on the parenting. All families need a lot of cooperation from family members and other adults who can have an influence.

Relatives, friends, and spouses influence your children even when they are talking only to you. Little radar ears pick up all conversation going by. Remember the topic is secondary—they are first interested in the feelings of the people. While keeping up with parenting obligations, you don't need an extra adult showing up your faults. On the other hand, an extra adult who comes to your aid with reinforcement when it seems parent abuse is likely, can be a real helping hand. And of course they should provide protection when their best friend is being mistreated, even by a child.

Hey! Don't talk to your mother like that!"

Friends should protect friends, that's obvious enough, but when the child is doing the mistreating, friends should be encouraged not to hesitate to establish and reinforce a respectful attitude in the child:

Jenny: "Mom, tie my shoe!"
Mom: "Just a minute. I'm talking."
Jenny: "Do it now!"
Eric: (Mom's close friend) "Don't talk to your mother like that, Jenny. Let your Mom finish, and what happened to 'please?'"
Mom: "Thanks, Eric, I can use that support now and then."

Eric wouldn't let a stranger barge in and make demands of his friend, say, at a restaurant, and he's not going to sit by when her child does it at home either.

Two adults can be stronger than one; they can also provide a model to child-ren about how the members of the family should treat each other. The careful-how-you-speak-to-your-mother remark, in addition to being a source of comfort to Mom, can also redirect a growing child blundering into accumulating guilt:

Kevin: "I'm going to watch TV now."
Mom: "How about your homework?"
Kevin: "Later. I've got plenty of time."
Mom: "Didn't you say your history paper was due tomorrow?"
Kevin: "Mom, you don't know anything about how long the paper will take."
Aunt Eileen: "Be careful how you talk to your mother. She's had

many years of school; I think she knows."

Kevin: "I'll do it when I'm ready."

Aunt Eileen: " Well, I can't ride you over to your soccer practice until your mother says you're ready."

Kevin: "You didn't even know about the history paper until Mom brought it up; what do you have to do with it, anyway?"

Mom: "Don't talk to your Aunt Eileen that way; she's concerned about you, too. Now get to that paper so you can make your soccer practice."

This struggle may not end here, but Mom and Aunt Eileen, standing up for each other, are not going to be a part of Kevin's divide-and-conquer strategy; they stay close and no abuse is tolerated.

Parent abuse: How friends can hinder

How does the parent abuse habit get started? Of course, a child's attitude comes from many sources, but again the relatives, friends, spouses, and extended family play a role from the beginning. They can make the effort to help, like Eric and Aunt Eileen, or, if they don't, they can be part of the problem.

Mike: "You can't find your keys? I can't believe it!"

Jane: "Just a minute, here they are."

Mike: "I swear, you would lose your head if you didn't..."

An adult game of "I-can't-believe-you're-such-a-klutz!" can be easily absorbed by the kids. In addition to sticking up for Mom, an adult friend or relative can unintentionally show the children how to abuse her. No one can watch everything they say, but friends of parents should keep in mind what examples are set for the kids. The best help a friend of a parent can give is to model respect for the one on the firing line.

In the car with Kevin and Jenny:

Aunt Eileen: "If you're going to look for a new car, you better take someone with you who knows something about it."

Mom: "I know something about it. I have three articles right here, and I   know the ratings."

Aunt Eileen: "Oh, well, from those articles, what do you think of the prices in these ads? "

> **Two adults can be stronger than one; they can also provide a model on how family members should treat each other.**

Aunt Eileen starts off negative but ends up asking about Mom's information. Now, Mom needs to return the favor:

Mom: "How is the one you have been holding up?"

If significant others are going to help, Mom's (or Dad's) model of respect for friends and companions needs to be part of the child's family experience. When Mom respects opinions of others, it improves the value of their opinions in the eyes of the kids. That will be a benefit when friends show confidence in Mom's ability in everything from driving to financial decisions. Everyone's ability to relate to the children on equal terms is increased. "What do you think about the prices in these ads?" sends a message not only *to* Mom, as a parent, that her thoughts are of value, but also to any little ears in hearing range.

Here's a good reason to sort out conflicts in private—away from the children. As with their own conversations, children have their "antennae out" and are more interested in what the conversations say about how the people feel about each other than in the content of the argument. Here's how the "little ears" can misunderstand a simple conversation:

Eric: "This car needs some work."

Jane: "Why don't you take it in Monday."

Eric: "Me? You're the one who drives it the most!"

Jane: "I have to get to work early. You just lounge around until 8:00 anyway."

Eric: "Hey, that cushy job of yours..."

Jane: "Wait, wait, let's get the car fixed, OK?"

You may think this argument is about car repairs and who should see that it gets done. But a child listening on the side doesn't understand—doesn't care to understand—the details of dropping a car off for repairs. The child is attending only the message about the opinion each person has of the other.

So after a simple disagreement about the car, Eric may be surprised to hear Jenny say: "You don't like Mommy, do you?"

"What! Of course I do, whatever gave you that idea?"

The misunderstanding a child gets from focusing on what seems to be the feelings the adults have for each other can be corrected. But the temptation to imitate what they have heard will linger on and show up as an argumentative attitude of their own! The impression on the child will only be corrected by future examples from Mom—and from the Erics, Aunt Eileens and other adults in the child's world.

Parent teams: How friends can help

Most encounters in parenting are first-time experiences. Even parents with many children are usually surprised at what the next child does. Whether you are on your own or in a partnership, a parent support group can be a great help. The other adults can create a sounding board for problems and provide the assurance that others have problems similar to yours. Even a reluctant spouse will develop new ideas and attitudes from a discussion group.

As your child wades through the teenage years, the support of other parents can strengthen your stand against heroes of violence in movies, parties with alcohol, and other perils and temptations coming up.

A few calls or an announcement in a school or church newsletter will produce other parents who are willing to be a part. Agreement on parental strategies is *not* a requirement. The opportunity to sort through common problems is what's important, and you will probably discover everyone is partly right. See the exercise on page 202 for suggestions about the ground rules.

For opening topics at meetings you could start with one habit or exercise from this book along with topics suggested by others.

People in your support group see your child less often than you do, so they can help you with new insights. Gradual changes taking place in a child going from age 2 to 12 are easy to miss. We often think of our children as about the same when changes are actually taking place every week and month! The parent support group can help a mom or dad who, not recognizing growth, continues old limits on responsibilities and opportunities. Timely changes would strengthen their son's or daughter's always-fragile self-worth.

Parents can lose influence just by neglecting the child's expanding areas of interest. A child's complaint of "nothing to do" should be taken as more than just a complaint about the lack of amusements. It could reflect a need for useful activities that are respected in his limited world. One fast way to alienate a member from a group (or family) is to not allow him to contribute when he's ready to!

A strange effect of sexism in our culture is that girls sometimes survive childhood better than boys because they make an earlier contribution to the family, particularly in the domestic chores. While "protecting" the male from drudgery, parents can run the risk of driving their son to find other activities that show he can "do something."

Threatened by his perceived "worthlessness," he will cast around for a way to show off—what will he find? Will it be a suggestion from his Mom or Dad? Or something away from his parent's influence and encouraged only by mischievous others?

Contrary to what your children say, you are still the main influence.

Competition for parental influence will come from a child's expanding circle of friends. While parents feel obligated to hold to limits that are not always popular, friends are likely to encourage a wide range of risky behaviors. Positive support is the major advantage parents have in competing against their child's friends who encourage and criticize without much thought.

> **One fast way to alienate a member from a group (or family) is to not allow him to contribute when he's ready to.**

But it can be tempting to continue support with no particular success in mind at all: "I think you're wonderful, you just make mistakes now and then." While support like this is often an important role for parents, it could be cruelly misleading preparation for an adult world that is less tolerant. Often, parental coaching needs to be realistic and helpful.

A parent support group can be helpful here as well. How are other parents reacting to new fads and habits? What *good* developments are they encouraging?

Growing up from age 2 to 12 opens new possibilities for games with parents. For example, "I-may-do-something-very-bad" is a game where the child *talks* about wild intentions because of the intense reaction his parents give to it. When you suspect this game is going on, you can try to inhibit your strong reactions to the verbal description of his intentions and concern yourself only with *performance*. These are important strategies to work out in your planning sessions and in your parent support group (you *are* planning one now, aren't you?). Without a strategy, you may help create a situation where your child finds it easy to "get through" to you by making a remark about some absurd behavior he has no intention of carrying out.

Getting a child to "talk right" sometimes becomes the goal of the parent and a power struggle for the child. Little talks may become unproductive because if the child starts to lose she can always agree to the demand without having to carry it through. Threats may be made, voices raised, and the child may get a good "talking to," but she will only learn to say what is expected and to avoid any genuine discussion of controversial topics.

As they grow, we must separate their responsibilities.

Children have to learn about two sets of responsibilities, their increasing personal responsibilities and their parents' slowly decreasing responsibilities for their child. First, the child's own responsibilities increase as they become old enough to care for themselves, then a share of the family domestic chores, and then their outside school and social responsibilities.

Most parents I know have found teaching the last of these—the social consideration—to be the toughest part of the personal responsibilities. While parents strive to create a pleasant atmosphere at home, the children don't seem to mind destroying it all just to get their way with the TV remote! And while the parents help their host when visiting relatives or friends, the younger kids have no thought for their social responsibilities, easily adding a sour moment over what chair they have at the dinner table!

"You have a responsibility to be considerate, too!" is a message and model parents need to attend frequently. It's a proud day at Aunt Ellie's when your son or daughter offers to help clean up after dinner! Was Dad's model also a part of this change?

The second set of responsibilities to be learned can also be a challenge. A parent's responsibilities for their child will conflict with the child's whims and demands. The authority will be better accepted if the communication and listening skills are kept sharp.

While parental roles change with situations as well as with the ages of the children, parents need to avoid feeling "inconsistent" when different roles are called for. Often a child's confusion over Mom's or Dad's responsibilities and changing attitudes can be erased by a frank explanation of their mixture of perspectives:

Chris: "Why can't we have the other cable channels? Everyone else has them."
Mom: "They cost more money. And not everyone has them. Parents in my group say they're too expensive, too."
Chris: "But we're missing all the good stuff!"
Mom: "You see plenty of TV with its violence and ...stuff. I want you to use some of your time for useful things, where you learn something."
Chris: "If you were my friend, you would get the other channels." (Sounds like a game of "If-you-loved-me,-you-would-serve-me.")
Mom: "Chris, I *am* your friend, but sometimes I have to be a parent who is a friend and also looks out for your future. It's not

easy doing both."

Chris: "Well, I'd be a lot happier friend if I had the other channels."

Mom: "Maybe so. But I have to be a parent who watches our money and watches out for your learning, as well as be a friend too. It's hard."

Does Chris understand all this about conflicting roles? I doubt it. But she does understand that Mom cares and understands, even when she will not provide what Chris wants.

Travis: "All the kids get so noisy at soccer practice. You're the coach, you should tell them to shut up!" (Sounds like a game of "You're-the-parent,-let-me-tell-you-your-job.")

Dad: "Sometimes I don't want to be the heavy. If there's nothing going on at the moment, they can let go a little."

Travis: "I try to tell them."

Dad: "Hard to control the whole group. Sometimes you should try going off with a friend and just doing a little passing practice until the next drill."

Travis: "You're more strict with me than you are with them!"

Dad: "It's different when they're not my children. Sometimes I worry more over how you are doing. For them I'm only the coach; for you I'm Dad."

College is coming. Why some quit and others stay the course

In my University of Maryland years as Associate Dean for Undergraduates, I gave a survey to over 500 drop-out students who came in to resign. Here is what I learned.

Only 10 percent of college dropouts have failing grades. Actually, the biggest dropout factors are wrong housing, acquired bad habits, poor care of their health, and bad time and money management—not grades.

> **Most dropouts work too many hours at an outside job far away from the campus.**

Living too far from campus while working long hours at an off-campus job ranks as the top factor in dropping out. If college life is limited to a job, driving, the campus parking lot, and classes, then cutting classes will be seem to be a good solution.

Bad personal habits are the next pitfall. If your usual caretakers are not around, you may feel, "Great. No more critics. I'm free to do what I want." But bad choices here have produced the poor health record of college students. You would think they would be the healthiest part of our population, but they aren't.

Drinking habits have an extra danger for college women. Fifty percent of women sexually assaulted on campus have been drinking at the time—making themselves more vulnerable—at least in the eye of the one doing the assaulting. The majority of women with unwanted pregnancies in the college-age group report they had been drinking at the time of the big "mistake."

Bad management makes the college dangers list because it's easy to become addicted to a job., to entertainment, computers or partying as well as the more familiar habits of drugs and alcohol. Skipping meals, sleep, or exercise makes getting sick more likely. When you start feeling bad, review your habits and your overdoses of salt, fat, sugar, and caffeine--they make you sleep poorly and feel tired and depressed.

College Can Be a SNAP

On the academic side, my advice to students and my own daughters boiled down to the letters in "SNAP" which can help the study and class time pay off in grades.

The "S" in SNAP stands for *Show Up*. Missing class is the best predictor of a slipping grade point average. Also, nearly all students who drop out begin the downhill slide by cutting classes.

The "N" in SNAP stands for *Notes*. You would think the high school advice of "take notes" would be in every freshman's mind, but when you look around in your college classes you'll see many students who don't take notes.

> **Never turn a page without writing down something.**

Notes not only provide valuable review, they keep your attention on the class and give you extra practice if you copy them neatly later.

The "A" in SNAP stands for *Active Studying*. Many of my students have said, "I can't believe I did poorly; I went through (stared at) all the pages assigned for the test!" If reading is the assignment, get active, take reading notes. Reading notes become a source of motivation and provide bench marks so you can pick up at the right place after the phone, coffee, or pizza interruption. Never turn a page without writing down something.

The "P" in SNAP stands for *Plan* ahead. Poor time management can be a big pitfall for students on their own for the first time. Look ahead and schedule your study time. Everybody needs party time, and you can't plan every minute, but a calendar will keep the priorities in order and, along with the rest of SNAP, you'll be ready for the tests.

For college freshmen, the first two semesters produce more dropouts than all the later years of college put together. After the first semester with big class projects and final exams, the second semester looms ahead. It's a crucial time for parents to send encouraging and positive signals to their student.

Samantha called home every week when she started college. Her Mom would respond, "Oh, Samantha, I hope you are well. We miss you so much. Your little sister is so lonely. She keeps asking, 'Is it time for Samantha's vacation yet?'"

These weekly tugs on the guilt strings were intended to let Samantha know she was loved, but she came to my office to fill out the paperwork to drop out and she completed the job.

Samantha's college career was short partly because her parents unintentionally emphasized family events that would make her homesick.

Keep the calls upbeat as much as possible, and the pressure low about jobs, money, and grades.

Most dropouts work too many hours at an outside job far away from the campus. In fact, that's the most outstanding difference between successful students and dropouts.

Sons and daughters who juggle jobs and school make their parents proud. But if the schedule gets too crowded with job and commuting, the college experience may be reduced to job, campus parking lot, and classes. No time left for meeting classmates, chatting with professors, or joining in the many campus activities.

Encourage your college-bound son or daughter to live and work close to the campus and work only the necessary hours at an outside job.

Another common reason for dropping out is loss of direction or enthusiasm for a planned major and career. Parents can help here also by talking over the majors represented in the early required courses and keeping the pressure to make an early decision low. One primary advantage of college is learning about the variety of life's opportunities.

Many colleges and universities have 100 or more majors, but few first-time students can name 20! No wonder over 90 percent of freshmen change their major along the way. Fifty percent will change majors more than once.

Students are often tempted to avoid this decision by leaving college for "a year off." But if college is viewed as a source of information about choices, then staying in makes sense. Little is lost by taking courses to explore the wide range of majors and careers before making this important decision. It's a long way from graduation to retirement.

An additional danger for students comes when their mailboxes fill with offers of merchandise and credit cards. Caution your college student to keep life simple with few obligations to make payments on cars, credit, and clothes.

Habits concerning health (sleeping, diet, and alcohol) and management of time and money, can also be dangerous pitfalls in the college journey. Most freshmen open a checking account and face the worries of a budget for the first time. They're on their own in budgeting their time, too.

Parents of teens with a year or two of high school left have time now to prepare their sons and daughters for the challenges of caring for themselves.

Passing along your parenting style

Of course you started passing your parenting style along as soon as you began parenting. You encourage some behaviors, model certain attitudes, discourage some habits, and support and nurture others. You started making the next generation of parents when you started child-rearing in this generation.

When your children are parents, you will coach them and help them. But you have been planting seeds for about two decades, and now they will start preparing yet another generation for parenting.

In these chapters I have advocated a practical approach to child-rearing. The kids have practiced your routines of conversation, your approach to both learning and teaching, your inclination to show how you like them, your model and discipline, and your attitudes toward the dangers of childhood.

> **Thoughtful and fair strategies will make your role more comfortable.**

My philosophy is that children and adults are more similar than we sometimes think. The most important similarities are that all of us deserve respect and room to learn and experiment.

The successful efforts of both adults and children need recognition and support to keep the progress of learning moving forward. For children, the feeling of self-esteem is still developing, and positive reactions from parents are especially needed for children to feel good about themselves.

Both adults and children deserve the same consideration when they make mistakes. Justification for punishment is not strengthened by pointing out the young age or small stature of the victim. Corrections, feedback, and a chance to make amends are still a big part of the parenting job.

Good listening habits are crucial to successful parenting. As the children grow, the communication becomes more complicated and the importance of listening skills grows accordingly.

Along with your successful parenting should come an enjoyment of the nurturing job. Thoughtful and fair strategies will make your role more comfortable. The critical addition is consideration of your own time and your need for support and respect.

Parents need to gather adults around them who will help with the parenting job by respecting and confirming parents' rights. Sometimes Grandma or Grandpa may need to be told, "Mom (Dad), it's harder for me if your remarks suggest to the children that I am not capable." If your spouse or a relative lives with you, it's all the more important that you show each other the respect you expect from the children and that you come to each other's defense and aid.

For the most part, your children will resemble you and the need to be a good role model makes parenting a hard job, but you are their best advantage because you're the one most interested in their welfare and you're close at hand. To raise good kids in these tough times, listen and teach, show them you like them, watch what's going on, model a good example, and cultivate your adult perspective.

We parents have an extra advantage: we learn well from each other. So as a final project, start that parenting group as suggested in this last exercise.

EXERCISE:
Parent teams: The ground rules for making them work

Parent support groups can provide comfort and a good sense of direction wih the proper ground rules. They might also serve as a sort of extended family for your child, adding a wider circle of positive adult influences and role models in your child's life.

The following concerns are suggested as the basis for an agreement on ground rules. The first get-together of the group should discuss ground rules and come to an understanding, if not an agreement, on how each issue will be handled.

Concerning trust:
1. Confidentiality.
2. Rules for telling stories on your children and repeating stories on others' children heard at group sessions.

Concerning consideration for others:
3. Controlling the air time.
    What is fair share?
    How will we police the air time?
    Air time on a hot topic.
4. Topic time and free time.

Concerning the topic:
5. Selecting topics.
6. The group is not an individual therapy session.
7. The group is not a couples therapy session.

Concerning general rules:
8. Degrading the children, even your own, is not allowed.
9. Members act on their own responsibility. For example, in dealing with schools, they do not act in the group's name.
10. Splitting the group is always acceptable. Sometimes when the ground rules are ignored, radical changes are necessary for your child's sake.

Suggestions for discussion topics

We're sure the parents in your group will come to each meeting with new concerns, problems, and topic ideas, but here are a few to get you started:

1. How do other parents handle meal-time problems such as getting the children to eat the right foods?
2. How do other parents handle the selection of TV shows? What shows do they recommend for children?
3. What about nightmares and fears? What do other parents do when their child has nightmares or is afraid to go to bed?
4. How do other parents handle problems such as lying?
5. How have others involved themselves and their children in civic, church or community activities?
6. Can other parents recommend books that have effective technique for managing key issues?

And for single-parent discussion groups:

1. How are others handling the role of *adult* and *parent*?
2. How have others talked over the issues of separation and divorce with their child?
3. How are others handling current love relationships while keeping a stable and predictable home life for their child?
4. How can I avoid making an enemy of my former spouse and competing with him/her. How can I work out the best interests of my child with him/her.

Behavior Chart (from page 67)

Date/Time	What happened?	Just before this?	What happened next?	Remarks

**If you enjoyed this book, please add
your review to its page on Amazon.com.**

Our mission is to help parents raise
their children to be competent
adults and lifelong friends.

Dr. McIntire can be reached by e-mail at
sumcross@aol.com

His column of helpful advice for parents
is archived at www.parentsuccess.com

Blog: www.rogermcintire.wordpress.com

Also by Dr. Roger McIntire
*Teenagers & Parents: 12 Steps to
a Better Relationship*
Proven and practical strategies for today's parents. This revised and updated edition includes strategies for dealing with a teen's use of cell phones, computers, and social media. Print: 9780961451943. $18.95. Also available as e-book at Smashwords.com and on Amazon.com.

www.ingramcontent.com/pod-product-compliance
Lightning Source LLC
Chambersburg PA
CBHW052021290426
44112CB00014B/2327